JERRELL TRULOVE

Friends First

First published by Jerrell Trulove 2021

Copyright © 2021 by Jerrell Trulove

All rights reserved. No part of this publication may be reproduced, stored or transmitted in any form or by any means, electronic, mechanical, photocopying, recording, scanning, or otherwise without written permission from the publisher. It is illegal to copy this book, post it to a website, or distribute it by any other means without permission.

Jerrell Trulove asserts the moral right to be identified as the author of this work.

First edition

ISBN: 978-0-578-86238-5

This book was professionally typeset on Reedsy. Find out more at reedsy.com

For my incredible wife whose support means the world to me, my daughter Madisyn who brightens my day, and my mother who is the strongest woman I've ever known.

"Press on in love'

Contents

Preface iii
Acknowledgement iv

I   Part One

1   Introduction 3
2   Things to Consider 14
3   The Fall 21
4   The Autopilot Love Experience 31
5   The Dating Conundrum 40
6   Love Is Scary 50
7   Marriage Is Serious 57
8   You Were Wrong 63
9   The Ex-Years 72
10 The Pool 77

II Part Two

11 More Things To Consider 83
12 The Friend Zone 86
13 The Anatomy of a Friend vs A Spouse 91
14 Can We Just Be Friends? 105
15 Friends First: Pros vs Cons 111
16 The 'No' List 127

17	The 'Yes' List	136
18	The Shift	143
19	Q & A	147
20	Love On Purpose	153
21	Change	156

Bonus Chapter	160
About the Author	162

Preface

If you:

are not looking for a serious relationship
enjoy having friends with benefits
want nothing more than to hookup
don't see the point in getting married

This book is not for you. Put it down, bookmark it, and come back to it later.

But if you:

desire to find a lifelong mate,
have a past of broken relationships and/or marriages
feel hopeless about finding the right person
want your next relationship to be your last relationship

This book was written specifically with you in mind.

I hope you enjoy this journey we're about to take.

Acknowledgement

This book could not have been made possible without the love and support of my incredible Wife. This book is a direct result of our relationship and further proof that she and I were meant to be together.

To the countless friends, family, and acquaintances who have listened to my crazy ideas, have offered their advice and input, and have supported me every step of the way. Thank you.

To my editor Vivian. Without you, this book would have been raggedy! Lol. Thank you for your patience, constant revisions, professionalism, and much more. Your hard work and dedication are priceless.

To my proofreader Diane. Thank you for your work, attention to detail, and for being my last-minute eyes and ears.

Last but not least, thanks to all of those who hope to find love in whatever corner of the world you find yourself. Thank you for reading and thank you for giving Friends First a chance.

I

Part One

1

Introduction

Choosing who you'll spend the rest of your life with is a decision that can make or break you. Regardless of the particulars of what you do, how old you are, or where you live, it is the single most important decision you can make during your time here on Earth. There's absolutely no way around it.

As extreme as this may sound, I believe that if you choose incorrectly, then your life can be destroyed before you even have the chance to step towards your full potential. The wrong person can sabotage your purpose in life, stress you out, discourage you, and otherwise stop you from achieving all the things waiting for you on the other side of success (whatever that may mean for you).

At best, you can look forward to a relationship mired with irritation, confusion, underlying feelings of unhappiness and resentment, or just a paralyzing level of averageness — all of which are situations we would rather avoid. On the other side of the coin lies a completely different experience.

If you choose the person you're meant to be with correctly, the possibilities are limitless. You'll experience an overwhelming feeling of peace and reassurance that you never knew was possible. You'll know — more than you've ever known anything else — that with this person by your side, you can accomplish everything you were meant to and much more. The right person in your life is a gift from the heavens and can take you to higher heights in every area.

All of this sounds great, right? I'd bet money that if you asked most people which experience they wanted, they'd choose, without hesitation, the latter. However, the problem lies in the fact that a lot of people have no earthly idea how to make this life-changing, all-important choice. The result of this lack of knowledge is usually an endless circle of trial and error that can result in bitterness, hopelessness, and a stoic indifference about something that should *never* be taken lightly.

Lots of people right now are hurting and need help. Man or woman, young or old, there are millions who just can't get this relationship thing figured out. They seem to attract the same type of person, fall in love at the drop of a hat, or stay in relationships that aren't serving them in a healthy way.

With the seriousness of marriage and relationships and the unique hurdles that we face in today's world, we simply cannot afford to get this relationship thing wrong. Not knowing what to do or how to go about selecting a mate can prove very, very costly. We cannot sit by and allow months and years of our lives to be wasted while we continue to fail over and over.

However, a lack of knowledge combined with social conditioning leads us to believe that we actually can afford to get it wrong or that whenever we're ready we can snap our fingers and find a mate with little to no effort. That's why so many people today can't explain why they're unable to find someone to spend the rest of their life with.

Everyone is searching for love and searching hard. They try online dating, hookup sites, websites, apps, reality TV shows, daytime talk shows, and more. But it makes sense. As humans, we are hardwired to desire connection with other people, and not knowing how to find that special someone can send us into a tailspin. If you also factor in the psychological issues people battle as a result of their pasts, then it becomes even more difficult to find the equation that gives us the answer we're looking for.

If we are unwilling to put in the work necessary to build rapport with others, have damage from our past, and don't have the self-awareness to know what part we play in making it all work, then we will sabotage ourselves at every turn, subscribing to dysfunction, lust, and denial, all the while calling it love. We will convince ourselves of something that simply isn't there. We'll experience the crushing blow of heartbreak and jump into another relationship before we even finish picking up the pieces from the last failure.

And this is where we find ourselves. Relationship after relationship, heartbreak after heartbreak, trying to figure it out but not knowing how. Attempting to get it right but falling short of the mark.

If you are looking for a spouse and don't want to fall victim to serial dating to find him or her; if you want to know with conviction that the person you are in an exclusive, committed relationship with is worth your time, effort, and energy; if you are tired of hookups that turn into flings that turn into breakups and you want to end the vicious cycle of highs and lows, then there's only one way to position yourself for success. You have to be friends first.

You have to abandon the outdated premise that most people unknowingly subscribe to that includes setting high expectations (which lead to disappointments); going on dates; overcommitting; and spending time, money, and energy on someone *before* truly getting to know them. You have to make the transition into giving the best parts of yourself to someone only *after* they have demonstrated that they are worth it.

It's not a popular concept, and for most, this idea might seem like an inconvenience more than anything. The information age has created an environment that makes finding the right person the right way a boring and uninteresting process. But being friends first as opposed to hoping you develop a lifelong connection after you've committed is pragmatic and intentional. It will help you take full control of any relationship rather than just "falling" into it, which is how a lot of us end up in messes.

This book won't give you a five-step formula that will guarantee you find a spouse in ninety days or less, and it's not about painting a perfect picture of the intricacies and nuances of sustaining a relationship in the twenty-first century. It's about learning what builds a strong, lasting partnership.

A big part of what allows people to heal from their past and move forward with optimism is simply learning more about relationships. The average person has probably never read a book, taken an online course, watched a YouTube video, or attended a seminar about how to be keen at developing and maintaining relationships. Most of us are out here with a blindfold on, feeling our way through things and hoping we don't get in harm's way. This book will help you take the blindfold off.

Friends First is a simple, straightforward account of many of the pitfalls and misconceptions about relationships, and it details the simplicity, practicality, and tangible benefits of establishing a meaningful friendship with someone as a prerequisite for entering into a committed relationship with that same person. It's about understanding compatibility and the plethora of things that make up a relationship.

This book is an introduction to a new approach for finding — and more importantly, sustaining — a relationship for life. *Friends First* is about setting the stage to make an intentional, mutual choice to start something new rather than fall into a situation based on emotional and sexual happenstance that most of us have gotten into at some point in our lives.

Friends First is dedicated to getting you out of the current culture of fly-by-night relationships and plugging into a culture of deliberate, on-purpose decision-making when it comes to this thing called love. If you're searching for an answer to the question "Why can't I figure this relationship thing out?" then there's a very simple solution. Be friends first.

***

Why am I writing this book, and why now? Because I've failed, and like most of us, I've failed big. Relationships have always been something I enjoyed, and deep down inside, I've always wanted to find "the one." My buddy Raul used to say, "You love love, don't you?" And he was right! But maybe I loved it a little too much.

Although I wasn't out in the streets sowing my royal oats everywhere, the problem is that I never had anyone sit me down and give me the inside scoop about how serious relationships are and how costly it can be if you choose incorrectly. What I've discovered for myself is that although I was fortunate enough not to marry the people who weren't right for me, I came very close. I have failed, and in my failures, I have learned why it's important to be intentional about who you let into your life. More importantly, I learned how to go about doing so.

My first failure came in high school. It was sophomore year and I had never had a "real" girlfriend in my life. There was a girl one year younger than me who liked me. We eventually started talking, and soon after I found myself in my very first "relationship" of sorts. Thinking back to that first one, I did everything wrong, even at my young age. I was never friends with the girl, and I never knew much about her other than the fact that she was tall and had a really, really big booty.

After about six months of being together, I began to hear rumors that she was cheating on me with another student at school, and I decided to break off the relationship and cut my losses. Although this one was short-lived, I understand that any number of other bad things *could* have happened while I was with this girl. The thought of that alone scares me sometimes.

My second failure came with my first serious relationship. I was a senior in high school at this point, and although I had lots of girls who "liked" me at the time, there was one particular girl who I was fond of. We were friends for a while and talked now and then on the phone until one day, I asked her when she and I would be together. Just like that, I had a girlfriend. Crazy, right?

Once again, I didn't know much about the girl other than the fact that she was my friend's cousin, she seemed to argue with her mother a lot, and she had an affinity for basketball just like me. That moment on the phone would be the beginning of a three-and-a-half-year relationship that didn't go the distance. I maxed out credit cards, spent money I didn't have, offered to let her move in, and did everything in my power to make her happy. Needless to say, the relationship ended, and I was left with that sinking feeling that we've all felt.

. My third failure was pretty much the same scenario all over again. After failure number two, I told myself that I wasn't going to jump right into something again unless I knew more about who I was considering. Well, in this case, I did know more about her — I just didn't know the *right* things about her that would have allowed me to make a more informed decision. Based on a few months spent together during the summer, we decided to embark on a long-distance relationship that ended in three cross-country moves, a daughter, several breakups, a proposal, and an eventual separation.

After my last failed relationship, I finally sat down and had a "come to Jesus" moment with myself. I had to admit that no matter how the relationship ended and no matter how much of a great guy I thought I was, I was *terrible* at finding, approaching, and connecting with the right person for me. Sure, I'm a fairly decent-looking guy and I've always felt like I was enough of a catch to find a new girlfriend fairly quick. But obviously something wasn't hitting home for me.

I knew all of the people I had gotten into a relationship with had good intentions and weren't evil people, but I was still missing a *huge* piece of the puzzle. As I thought about it more and more, I realized that I never took any *real* time to discover if *any* of the people that I committed to being in a relationship with were truly worthy of my time, money, energy, affection, and consideration.

I finally understood that I was following a formula for disaster. I was leaving out the most important component necessary to ensure I wouldn't find myself single again in a couple of years. I never took the time to be friends with any of them first. Granted, we had some level of chemistry, and we enjoyed spending time together. Yes, we knew about each other's pasts and families in a general sense. And yes, we could spend hours on the phone, and at times we could enjoy each other's company without a care in the world. But looking back at all of my relationships, I barely scratched the surface and it proved to be disastrous.

I'm completely aware that there are couples out there who decided to get married just a handful of months after meeting each other. I'm also aware that there are lots of couples who, after following that formula, are still together. While I'm ecstatic that they've found that special someone, I think they are the exception to the rule.

When you enter into a relationship too hastily, you are gambling with your time, your sanity, and potentially your life. You might say that I'm being a bit extreme, but divorce rates would say otherwise. According to the American Psychological Association, 40 to 50% of married couples divorce. This suggests that people aren't taking the time to get to know who they're dedicating their life to. Lucky for me, the relationships that weren't meant to be never went the distance.

Unfortunately, there are others who can't say the same. My past is littered with a handful of serious relationships, a few dating failures, some summer flings, and an ocean of bad decisions made in haste or lust. Yes, these experiences helped mold me into the person I am today, and they helped shape the expectations I have for relationships moving forward. But the thought I had in those moments and continue to have to this day is that there has to be a better way. There *has* to be a better way. Failing miserably can't be the only formula for success in relationships, can it? Should you have to endure years and years of bad decisions to finally find someone that fits the mold? Do we have to make up and break up over and over to finally get it right?

Well, the answer is a resounding no. We don't have to continue to endure pain before we are able to experience the pleasure of a fulfilling relationship, and I was able to ultimately find my own relationship success within the confines of a friendship.

I met my wife in 2008 while she was studying abroad here in America. We were both seeing other people at the time, but we still became great friends. Years later after she returned home to London, we reconnected online, and without realizing it, that's when our journey began. I discovered that when you take the time to truly embrace the idea that a lifelong partnership can and should be born from a friendship, you set yourself up for success in a way that makes so much sense. A way that feels natural and logical and doesn't contain a lot of the pitfalls that traditional dating does.

No, it won't be easy. Yes, there will still be hurdles to overcome, as in any relationship. But the foundation that true friendship establishes is one meant to withstand the test of time. Without knowing it, I became friends first with my wife over the course of an eighteen-month period after we reconnected. We were able to open up and be honest about who we were, where we were in life, what we had been through, and where we were heading in the future. Neither of us had to pretend or perform for the other person. We became friends with no strings attached. After all was said and done, we discovered mutual feelings that laid the framework for a long-distance relationship that led to our marriage today.

After so much failure, I finally uncovered the truth. The way to win in a relationship is to not try winning at it. Trying to win is comparable to putting the cart before the horse. The way you win at relationships is by winning at friendship first. If you can win at that, then committing to someone will be one of the easiest and best decisions you'll ever make. My wife and I won at friendship and it's what set the stage for our marriage today. No pretending. No being something we both weren't.

In case you hadn't been told, relationships are serious business. They aren't harmless connections we make with people. They aren't something you can joke around with and come out clean on the other side. Relationships can be the catalyst for transforming your life, or they can be the beginning of your downfall.

As grateful as I am for what I've learned, I can't help but ask myself what would have happened if I had real friendships first in my past relationships. What if I had known that having a few things in common wasn't enough, and that liking the same music was more of a coincidence than a clear indicator that someone might be a candidate for future consideration? What if I had taken ample time to ask the right questions, have more conversations, and dig deeper? What if I had been *real* friends first with any of the women that I called my girlfriend? Where would I be today?

Where would you be?

This book is divided into two parts. Part I addresses a lot of the pitfalls and stumbling blocks we experience in relationships and also introduces new metaphors, ideas, and concepts that will help you to approach your next situation with a clear mind. We must address these problem areas first to lay a new foundation of knowledge and self-awareness that we can build on. Each chapter ends with reflection questions so you can see where you're making mistakes in your relationships.

Once we reach a baseline of understanding in Part I, Part II is where everything falls into place. Part II introduces the idea of Friends First — why it's effective, what you can expect while you're implementing this plan, and why the result is worth the effort. In the end, you should feel a sense of closure from your past, focus for where you are currently, and optimism for your future. Let's dive in.

2

Things to Consider

Before you dive into the pages of this book, there are a few things you should consider or at least be made aware of. The goal here is not for you to agree or disagree with the following, but rather to make you think. To start an internal dialogue about relationships and introduce ideas that perhaps you hadn't taken the time to ponder.

When it comes to relationships, we can be so quick to depend heavily on our emotions instead of focusing on logical and rational ideas, concepts, and signs. Friends First is about doing just that. Yes, relationships do involve emotion, love, and feelings, but oftentimes we completely abandon reason and make lifelong decisions based solely on how we feel and not what we know. The following points are meant to inject more knowledge into your relationship equation and add new concepts to your dating lexicon.

Compatibility > Love

Tina Turner said it best. What's love got to do with it? Simply put, love is not enough, or love shouldn't be the most important factor in your relationship. To commit to someone, you need to love them on some level, but unless you married your high school sweetheart and are *still* married to that one person, you have had a first-hand account of how deceptive, powerful, and hypnotic the allure of love can be.

At one point, you have probably been head over heels for someone, going out of your way to do everything in your power to treat them the best you possibly can, all in the name of love. And after a monumental effort on your part, you discover that the person you gave your all to wasn't the one. It's a crushing feeling. Like having the weight of the ocean on your chest. Afterward, you began thinking thoughts like, "Am I enough?" or "How could things end up like this?" And of course, the all-too-familiar, "Maybe I could have done more?"

Most of us have been there. Again, we tend to focus mostly on how we feel and not what we know. Compatibility, however, is a different situation. It's knowing things like how someone wants to raise their kids and what they want to teach them. It's knowing if the person you're with has the maturity to admit when they are wrong. It's knowing if someone is equipped to love you (here's the kicker) the **way** you like and **need** to be loved. It's knowing that the person you are with has your best interest at heart and shows it both in words and action. The point is that although love is important, it does not guarantee compatibility, which, as we know, is a better indicator of relationship success. *But* compatibility will almost always lead to love if it's allowed to grow.

To connect the dots, remember that one of the goals of becoming friends first is to inject more "knowing" into our decision-making and a little less "feeling." And that knowledge comes from tangible things you have seen and can measure over time. You may love someone for one reason or another, but can you depend on them? Can they play a role in helping you achieve your goals and dreams? On a basic level, do you two fit well together? Love does *not* guarantee that you will mesh well, hence why many people experience breakups in their lifetime.

Another way to think about this is that you can fall in love with who you think someone is, but you are compatible with who someone truly is after you get to know them. If you discover you are in sync after getting to know someone, it's almost an absolute that love will grow from that. How could you not love someone who continues to add value to your life after the honeymoon phase has worn off?

Dating Doesn't Work

Dating does *not* work. I repeat. Dating does *not* work. You may be thinking, "But I found my wife because of a blind date that my friend convinced me to go on," or, "I went on a few dates with a guy I liked and three years later, here we are." That's all fine and dandy, but the real question is: what about the dozen or so failed dates before the one that finally worked? What about all of the people you had to siphon through to finally arrive at the person who it made sense to be with? How do you explain all of the money, time, energy, and resources you had to give up to "finally" find that special someone?

Although you ***eventually*** found your spouse, the point people miss is that it didn't have to cost you so much in the process; the process costs more than you realize. You could have still had the same outcome without the negative side effects of dating and seeing what that other person was all about. You could have learned the lessons without the commitment, which we'll get into more in Part II.

Granted, there are some benefits to dating, as it does help you learn more about what you do want by experiencing what you don't want. But if we're honest and take inventory of our relationships, we'll discover that these are all things we can discover about a person without going on a date with them or dating them over the course of several weeks, months, or years.

You might say that you don't mind dating, that it's fun for you to engage with others or that there's no harm in grabbing a drink or dinner to test the waters. However, for those of you looking for a better way but not knowing how to articulate how you feel, there's a simple solution. Stop dating people and focus on becoming friends first. If dating hasn't worked up until this point, why keep following the same flawed system?

Purpose as a Prerequisite

You may have heard that people don't change. While you may or may not agree with this, one thing that is usually bound to change in someone's life is their purpose. There are times in our lives where we discover our purpose, and that causes us to change our habits, our social circles, our values, our language, our priorities, and much, much more. Purpose can oftentimes be a catalyst for success in any relationship, or it can be a detriment just the same.

Let's consider Greg as an example. Greg attended a four-year college, graduated with a bachelor's in criminal justice, and is currently working as a dispatcher at the local precinct. He makes decent money and enjoys a somewhat comfortable life. One day, Greg's grandmother passes, and after hearing the news, he feels a deep sense of aimlessness. He realizes he is unhappy with his career and has been for some time.

Thinking long and hard about what would fulfill him, Greg realizes that he's always loved photography and has always thought it might be cool to buy a camera just for fun. It's at this moment that things change for Greg. He begins using his free time to research cameras and lenses to buy, invests in new gear, attends conferences when possible, does photo shoots in his free time, buys a new computer to help with editing, and much more. In essence, Greg's focus, time management, and circle of friends start to change, and the life he knew before is no longer his reality. Greg has found his purpose, and his life will never be the same. If Greg is in a relationship as he discovers his purpose, the way he and his partner handle the changes in lifestyle that will occur as a result will make or break their relationship.

When qualifying someone to spend the rest of your life with you, you need to make sure that you factor in purpose. Think about it. Whether it be launching a new business, starting a clothing brand, developing an app, or buying investment properties, every single one of us has a purpose. Every single one of us has certain gifts, and every single one of us has something we are meant to do during our lifetime. For those of you who have found your purpose or are in the process of discovering it, having this goal or skill you're trying to master is at the center of most of the decisions you make.

Likewise, if the one person on earth you choose to spend the rest of your life with can't or won't help you to realize and achieve your purpose, then what real benefit can they be to you? If your lifelong partner plays no active role in helping you achieve your lifelong goals, then one of three things will invariably happen: you will give up your purpose to make your partner happy, you will give up your partner to pursue your purpose, or you will try to juggle between both and take ten times longer to reach success in either area.

In Greg's case, the person he is in a relationship with will have a choice to make. Will they support him? Will they complain that he doesn't have enough time for them now? Will they help push him forward, or will they hold him back? Inversely, the same questions can be asked about Greg in terms of how he may react to what his partner is doing or trying to achieve. The point is that if you and the person you end up with aren't tuned into what each other's purpose is and aren't helping each other achieve that, then trouble will likely be on the horizon at some point. Prioritizing purpose leads to success in relationships.

It Takes More Time

I think most of us can agree that taking longer to get to know someone is never a bad thing. If we look back at our failed attempts at forever, we always realize we didn't take things slowly enough. The point is that a few months is never going to be enough time to truly get to know someone on a level that can justify a lifelong commitment. That might hurt to hear, but it's true.

Yes, some people end up getting married months after meeting, and yes, some of them are still married to this day, but they got lucky. Plain and simple. For the rest of us, that short timeline just won't work. For all intents and purposes, let's say that during the period of a few months, you talked to someone day and night and learned the innermost workings of their thoughts, feelings, emotions, their past, and so on. Great! That might work, *but!* The problem is that most people will *never* do that. Most people will spend the first few months of a relationship having lots of sex, avoiding tough conversations, and then deciding that forever just makes sense.

There are a large number of people who are simply trying to get in where they fit in and are simply trying to smash first and ask questions later. That's why we are where we are today. The reality that we fight so hard against is that lifelong relationships need more time to germinate before they can sprout into something great. Depending on who you are, it may take a few months or maybe even a few years before you can find forever with someone, but the fact of that matter is that it just takes more time. Trust me.

These ideas will be mentioned here and there throughout the pages of this book and are meant to give you a new way of looking at relationships. If we aren't careful, we can become slaves to our emotions, and if we aren't careful, we can find ourselves confused, frustrated, and angry at the things that we have said and done, wishing we could turn back the clock. Now that we've taken a moment to introduce some new ideas into your mindset, this will set the tone for the rest of the entire book. There are going to be some things you agree with, and some things you think are flat-out crazy. You've been warned.

However, the point is not to get you to agree with me. The point is to get you to think. When it comes to relationships, a large number of us simply don't take the time to think things over, and it's costing us dearly. And in this particular case, the old saying rings staggeringly true. If you know better, you do better.

3

The Fall

Before we can address what you may or may not have done to get you where you are, let's first talk about where you are and what's happening to you right now. If you are currently single, then at this very moment, you are experiencing or have experienced what I refer to as "the fall." Whether it happened six years ago or yesterday, at the end of every relationship is the inevitable fall. This is where you have severed the relationship's ties, and both of you are sent into a freefall from the top floor of the structure you built together. Some fall from hundred-story high-rises, and some people fall from two-story shacks, but all in all, you still fall, and falling will always hurt. Falling will always cause unwanted consequences, and falling will never be something that any individual looks forward to. Period.

Think about what it feels like to fall for a second. Words that might come to mind are fear, uncertainty, panic, distress, and anything synonymous with not knowing the outcome of what's happening. In a word, falling is scary. But what happens when we take the fall? When we fall, our natural response is to grab anything and everything we can on the way down. It's a reflexive, self-correcting action that aims to soften the blow that awaits us at the bottom.

Matters of the heart are no different. When a relationship ends and we are thrust into the fall, we tend to claw, scrape, and grab at anything we can to stop the falling and return to a sense of stability and control. Common things we grab for during the fall are attention, sex, affection, power, or a sense of closure.

The problem is that on the way down, we grab these things in a panic, creating an unhealthy, usually toxic connection to what we grab. For example, during the fall post-relationship, you might decide to grab a hold of sex and start sleeping with several people to feel a sense of control and comfort during an otherwise stressful and scary situation. You're still falling, but now, at least, you have some temporary comfort. During the fall, you might also panic at the thought of being alone again after so many years of companionship, and in a manic state of survival, you grab painkillers to numb yourself to the thoughts that plague you day in and day out. The thing is that when we're in the fall, we'll grab whatever we can get our hands on to avoid what is waiting for us at the bottom. We will grab it and hold onto it tight, even if it leaves us worse off.

In essence, we pick the lesser of two evils and trade the short-term pain of the fall for a toxic reaction that could cause long-term effects. When you're in the fall, the only thing on your mind is trying to keep yourself from hitting the bottom, and you'll do it at almost any cost.

Think for a second and ask yourself...have you grabbed for something while you were in the fall? Have you grabbed for something this month? This week? Today? Maybe you sent an inappropriate text, had a one-night stand, got high as a form of temporary escape, or even called your ex and begged them to take you back. That's you attempting to avoid what's waiting for you at the end of the fall.

So what *is* waiting for you after the fall? What's on the other side of the pain associated with another failed relationship? What are we so afraid of? Well, what makes the fall so tough to handle is not the fall itself, but our perception of how the fall will affect us. You aren't afraid of having to start over from the ground floor again — you're afraid you won't be able to begin again, or you're afraid you won't be able to find someone else. The fear of the fall is usually all in our minds.

If I asked you objectively, "Will you survive this breakup?" almost every single person would answer with a simple "yes." But in the heat of the moment, when we're in the middle of the fall, all is lost, and we have to do whatever we can to avoid the pain.

But the fall is a good thing if used correctly. When used correctly, the fall is what prepares us for the next relationship, and it causes us to make the necessary adjustments for the future. When we fall, we must try our best not to give in to the impulse to grasp at straws on the way down. We do this by keeping the end in mind and understanding that now we are one step closer to making better decisions and finding the person we are truly meant to be with. Always keep the end in mind.

What happens when you hit rock bottom after you fall from grace? After every fall, we are given the unique opportunity to perform crucial self-assessment that is the key to moving forward. Once you're at the bottom and the dust settles, you now have that much-needed pause to reflect, assess, and begin to move again, something that the "questions to ask yourself" sections at the end of each chapter will help you with. The problem is that the things we cling to during the fall are what distract us from healing properly.

Think of It This Way...

If you had a freak accident, fell, and broke your ankle, the *last* thing you would do is get right back up and start climbing again. Think about it. If you felt that pain in your right ankle, the last thing on your mind would be, "Let me get back up and get active as soon as possible." You would be *very* careful in your next moves. Not only for the next few moments, but the coming weeks, months, and possibly years.

On a more immediate note, you would first lie there and take a good self-assessment. You'd take a moment to see what else you injured during the fall. You'd look around to see where your cell phone was. You'd call a friend or yell for help. You would go to a doctor or physical therapist to get a diagnosis for your injury, get a prescription, get an x-ray, and get a cast if needed. You would walk differently and think differently for the next four to six weeks. You would do whatever it took to make sure that you healed properly from the fall, and you'd approach the aftermath with patience and tact.

I know this is quite a lengthy example, but it goes to show you the dozen or so steps you would take in the aftermath of a fall to make sure you could return to life as normal. You would do these things every single time.

But what do most of us do in relationships? Lots of us would have grabbed onto several things during the fall and added insult to injury. Secondly, after the fall, a good number of us would get right back up and hobble into the next situation, still severely injured both psychologically and emotionally. We'd stand back up, ankle be damned, and continue to walk down the street with a massive limp.

Now picture, if you will, the bustling downtown area of a major metropolitan city and imagine if you saw everybody attempting to walk around with broken ankles. It would be the most painfully awkward experience. Yet in our present-day society, that's exactly what you would see in terms of the emotional landscape. People walking through their pain instead of staying still and healing.

Injuries, Not Baggage

There's a new term that needs to be introduced, and that term is *injuries*. You see, we've always heard that when it comes to relationships, a lot of us carry around baggage. However, that term isn't entirely accurate. Extra baggage in a relationship is never a good thing. This can include bad habits, emotional ties to people, children, financial burdens, and more. If you think about it, though, baggage is something you can drop off eventually. I don't think most people suffer from extra baggage, but rather injuries that haven't been properly healed or acknowledged.

When you suffer an injury, it affects the way you live for the next several weeks, months, and sometimes for the rest of your life. An injury, depending on the severity, will not only affect you but everyone around you. Injuries result in frequent doctor visits, medication, rehabilitation, and most importantly, scars — scars that you will have for the rest of your life and are clear indicators of past hurt.

In relationships, we either don't take the proper time to heal or we don't acknowledge that we're even injured in the first place. We walk into our next one severely impaired and wondering why we fall short of the mark. We have to be aware that every single time we fall, there *is* an injury that takes place, even if your relationship was short-lived. Even if you try to convince yourself that you were just friends with benefits. You may not realize it, but you *did* get injured, and every single injury we experience that goes unchecked compounds onto the next one, causing us to fall over and over again.

A classic case of this is the rebound experience a lot of us have gone through where we hop into a new relationship thinking that it will heal us from our most recent injury. But then we discover that we constantly compare our present to our past and that we are not emotionally equipped to give ourselves completely to our new partner in a way that will serve the relationship well. We think that just because we "block" the memories of our last relationship, all is well. And as you can probably attest, we are almost always wrong.

We are dealing with injuries, not baggage. Permanent scars that live with us, not extra weight we can discard. Not an inconsequential fling. You need to always be aware of where you stand as far as healing from the past so that you don't repeat the same mistakes and hurt those who had nothing to do with you falling. When you don't give credence to exactly how your past injuries shape your current reality, you are setting yourself up to fail before you start.

This is how we move forward from the pain of the fall and begin to make inroads into relationships that are formed from a healthy place instead of from a place of need or ignorance.

Trauma

When exploring the idea of the fall and after taking the time to explore our injuries, we cannot move forward without also addressing an issue that has a major effect on our lives: trauma. Everyone experiences trauma in some form or fashion, and these instances of trauma, insignificant as they may seem, are the events that shape the way we react to and interact with the environment around us and cause us to do things we may not even realize or understand.

Understand that although not all trauma is created equal, trauma is trauma. It can be a single, devastating life event such as the passing of a relative, or it can be something that happens gradually over the course of months or years, like the way you were raised or the environment in which you grew up. Either way, trauma is something that we must become aware of and fix.

For any relationship to work, trauma *must* be addressed and dealt with. Again, this is one of those things that we cannot and will not ever be able to get around. The trauma in your life could be the thing that makes you ultra-aggressive or unnecessarily shy, it could be the thing that gives you that attitude that people hate, and it could be the thing that contributes to the behaviors and actions that can be or have been devastating to your relationships.

To dive deeper, let's consider Frank as an example. Frank is very conflict-avoidant and has issues with self-esteem, asserting himself, and making eye contact with others. Frank has been like this for as long as he can remember and has never asked himself why. This is just how he is. When it comes to relationships, Frank's shy nature has always caused problems, as the women he's involved himself with have accused him of being indifferent, uninterested, emotionless, or just plain afraid to speak up when the situation calls for it.

Having never asked himself why he is the way he is, Frank continues the same behavior, expressing the old adage, "This is how I've always been." One day, when Frank takes the time to honestly look at his life and attempt to assess why he exhibits these behaviors, he realizes that it's because of the trauma he's experienced. As a child, he was raised by loud and abrasive parents who groomed him to shut up and follow instructions. They never gave him the opportunity to voice how he felt or why. It was a "do as I say or be punished" dynamic that did not serve him well.

Growing up, Frank began to feel as though his thoughts and feelings weren't important or valued, and thus developed a habit of suppressing those same thoughts and feelings in order to avoid conflict and maintain peace. To this day, he exhibits this behavior at work, while hanging with friends, and in his personal, intimate relationships. Now that Frank is finally aware of the "why," he can now focus on the "how" required to heal from this trauma and be a more effective communicator. Whether it be therapy or simply talking through how he feels with his partner, he has now given himself the tools needed to heal from his personal trauma and move forward in a positive, healthy way.

Why are we talking about Frank, and why is this important? It's important because just like Frank, we all have gone through some form of trauma. In a lot of cases, it contributes to or multiplies the severity of our injuries and can be what is preventing us from maintaining relationships or healing from our previous ones.

THE FALL

When we experience the fall, it's never a good thing, but trauma can sometimes be at the root of why things fell apart and why we're experiencing the fall in the first place. When we are with someone for life, we need to be aware of our past trauma and their past trauma. We need to be willing to take steps towards healing those issues. We need to be willing to talk through these issues as a team and attack the behaviors, not each other. If not, then when those issues surface — and they will — we will be ill-equipped to figure out why, and we will continue to repeat this cycle until we address what needs our attention or the relationship falls apart.

When it comes to the end of any relationship, the hardest part is dealing with the fall. The thing we must battle with the most is resisting the urge to grab anything on our way down. While grabbing something during the fall may feel safe, it usually adds insult to injury. The best thing you can do is simply fall. Don't deny it and don't try to justify making rash decisions because of it. Let yourself feel all the sadness, anger, and regret that the end of a relationship can bring and position yourself mentally to learn rather than to resist.

When you fall, your primary objective should be to come to terms with the fact that you are falling, and that there is a lesson to be learned from it. When you do hit the bottom, you must properly assess the damage by doing some self-reflection, addressing what trauma you have or may have suffered, and ensure that you can move forward from a place of strength and awareness. And part of being able to move forward from a place of strength is understanding more about how society views love and how we put ourselves into a position to fall in the first place.

Questions to ask yourself:

1. How did I handle the last time I experienced the fall?
2. Did the way I handled the fall cause even more damage?
3. What unchecked injuries do I have from past relationships?
4. Have I ever taken the time to address my past trauma?
5. Has my past trauma ever affected the outcome of a relationship?
6. What have I learned from the fall that will set me up for success in the future?

4

The Autopilot Love Experience

If someone asked you why you thought relationships fail so often, what would you tell them? Money fights? Ignoring the red flags? Impatience? These could all be causes, but have you ever considered that there might be a bigger picture we haven't looked at? Something deeper that goes unnoticed and unrecognized? Why do we fall again and again?

I've come up with a theory that I call the "autopilot love experience." Simply stated, it's an explanation for why relationships fail and is something that we've all experienced without even realizing it. It's more of a silent killer, and when it kicks in, it strikes with deadly force before you've fully realized what's happened. Understanding autopilot love and what it looks like will help you stop it in its tracks if you see yourself falling into it in the future.

Below you can see a timeline of exactly how we experience autopilot love.

Meet > Triggers > 'Love' > Pavlovian response > Autopilot

Autopilot love is a simple set of stages that result in a failed relationship that should have never begun in the first place. It's deceptive because autopilot looks, feels, and sounds just like the real thing. You meet someone, they trigger you, you feel as though you love them, your Pavlovian response kicks in, and from there it's a waiting game until the relationship falls apart. Now that we know the what, let's dive into the how and why.

You Meet Someone

You meet someone. Simple enough, right? You're at a social event, a brunch with a group of friends, or a wedding reception. The simple fact is that you meet someone. You exchange information and start contacting each other. At this point, nothing has happened yet, and with the right awareness, you could walk away unscathed. However, you don't have that awareness yet. Now, this doesn't mean that you're hellbent on making this person your spouse and proposing next week, but it does mean that there is some sort of connection that you two entertain at some level. During this period, your intentions are irrelevant. You could be taking it slow, or you could even be trying to hit it and quit it, but these details are minutiae. Whether you talk for a few days, a few weeks, or a few months, the fact of the matter is that you met someone.

Triggers

A new phrase that has recently wiggled its way into the common lexicon is the word "triggered." In its most understood meaning, it describes a situation in which someone says or does something that strikes a nerve with someone else and the offended (or "triggered") person reacts accordingly. When it comes to relationships, as you may have already guessed, we can become triggered just the same.

However, relationship triggers have an entirely different context and result. Relationship triggers are things that someone else says or does in a casual friendship or relationship that cause us to accelerate through the friendship and factfinding phase or eliminate it all together. They tap into a primal response that can short-circuit our intentions and make us do and feel certain things without realizing it.

Relationship triggers could include physical appearance or how attractive someone is, money and financial stability, charisma and popularity, sexual prowess, the number of things in common you have, and the list goes on. The point is, we all have triggers. When discovered, these triggers make us lean in when in fact we should be taking a step back. These triggers can vary in number and strength, and no two triggers are created equal. For example, one of your triggers might be someone who dresses well, but on a scale of one to five, you might give that a two.

On the other hand, if someone can do acrobatics in the bedroom, you're giving that person a five almost immediately. So it's a combination of how many and also which triggers get set off that determines how you react when they pop up. I'll never forget back in college when a buddy of mine told me the story of a phone call he got from a girl he had known for a few months. They had sex, and the next day during that call she told him she thought he was her soulmate because he made her orgasm more times than any guy she had ever been with. My buddy was speechless as he barely knew her and wasn't really interested on *that* level. Triggered in a nutshell.

What tends to happen is that when triggered, most of us take it as a sign that there must be something deeper about this person that we need to explore through the guise of a relationship. This is the moment where we mess up. If you don't get this part right, then you will typically play out the rest of the timeline in its entirety, right on schedule. How long does it take before someone can set off your triggers? There's no real answer. If you have sex with someone quickly, it can happen within a few days or weeks, but if you wait longer, it can happen in a few months. But again, time is irrelevant. The fact of the matter is, you got triggered.

Feelings of Love

After you've been triggered, what happens next is the love phase. At this point, you begin to feel very strong feelings towards this person based on the amount and strength of your triggers, not because of how compatible you two are in reality. You begin to have conversations with yourself or your friends about how you think you might be in love (with someone you barely know, by the way). You begin to think about this person every day, compare and contrast them to your past relationships, wonder how you ever lived without them. You tell yourself, "This could be it."

This part of the timeline blindsides most people, and they simply give in to it without much resistance. At this point, we are operating primarily on an emotional level and have convinced ourselves that what we feel is real and therefore must be valid. It's pretty much a done deal at this point. By now you are in a full-blown relationship and have told the world. You're in love.

Pavlovian Response

In the late 1800s, physiologist Ivan Pavlov began experimenting with dogs and their salivation response to food. During his experiment, he discovered that not only would these dogs salivate when food was placed in front of them, but the dogs would salivate when they heard the footsteps of his assistant who was bringing them the food. This prompted him to dig deeper.

What he learned after a series of experiments was that after introducing a neutral stimulus such as a buzzer, a flashing light, or a bell before presenting the food, the dogs would eventually react to the stimulus. He would show them the stimulus and then give them the food over and over until eventually the dogs would respond to the stimulus the same way they would respond to the food. He called this a conditioned response, also known as a Pavlovian response — a response that is learned over time and becomes automatic. The key takeaway from this is the term *automatic*.

What does this have to do with relationships? Whenever the word *love* is introduced into a relationship, it changes everything — regardless of time or circumstances. As soon as we have convinced ourselves that we "love" someone, and when we believe in our hearts that what we are feeling for this person must mean something deeper, we fail to understand that society and human nature have unknowingly equipped us with a set of conditioned responses, much like the dogs in Pavlov's experiments. When we "love" someone, there are a set of behaviors and habits that we exhibit *automatically* without even realizing it. The way this manifests itself varies but will typically look and sound the same.

- We love each other, so let's move in together.
- I love him, so I want to sleep with him.
- I love her, so I'm going to cosign on this car with her.
- We love each other, so we have unprotected sex.
- We love each other, so let's have a baby together.
- We love each other, so let's open up a joint bank account.
- And the list goes on....

When it comes to love, there is a myriad of things we do for the sake of how we feel. Regardless of how insane, toxic, risky, or dysfunctional these actions are, we do them without any regard to what the fallout will be, throwing caution to the wind every chance we get. We'll call in sick to work, we'll spend money we don't have, we'll lie, and we'll put our health and sanity on the line simply because of that four-letter word. What's most alarming is that while we're in the eye of the storm, we won't even recognize what's happening.

Autopilot Love

Planes today are mostly flown on autopilot. Pilots in the cockpit are in the driver's seat but mostly monitor and observe what is happening without full control at all times. Although autopilot is amazingly convenient and intuitive, what would happen if a pilot needed to make an emergency landing while descending into a city because of engine failure or the landing gear not deploying correctly? The pilot would take full control of the plane and land the plane to the best of his or her ability. But more specifically, the pilot would have to rely more on what he knew and less on what he felt at that moment. He may be afraid, but when the rubber meets the road, a pilot has to *know* what he is doing. Otherwise, he is putting lives in danger because of his lack of knowledge. So many of us, after traveling through this timeline, experience the highs and eventual lows of autopilot love.

Much like the airplane flying high in the sky, when we feel love there is usually a sense of happiness, peace, and stability when we are deep in the throngs of our newest relationship. We're happy, we feel like we're on top of the world, and there's nothing that could go wrong. We are posting on social media four times a week, we wear matching sweaters on Christmas Eve, and we can't wait to come home to this person every single day.

Autopilot love is an experience where we are so deep into a relationship that we become numb to the fact that we are ill-equipped to handle the unavoidable hard times that every relationship faces. Autopilot love is how people end up married after six months of knowing each other, and it's also how that same couple ends up on a daytime talk show asking for advice to help solve an issue in their relationship that can't be fixed.

One time on a daytime talk show, there was a couple who was asking for advice because they couldn't agree on whether or not they should have kids. While I was watching the show, the only things I kept thinking to myself were, "How in the world are you involved exclusively with someone for two years and you don't agree on whether or not you should have kids? How in the world are you on the cusp of marriage when you two are so diametrically opposed on an issue that is of exponential importance in a relationship? How on earth have you two made it this far without having the answer to this question laid out in plain English?"

The answer to all these questions is very simple. Autopilot love. Autopilot love is what causes people to get a divorce after fifteen years of marriage, a house, a few cars, and several children. Autopilot love presents the façade that as long as all is well in our lives, we will be together forever. But much like the pilot who must take control of a plane, if we have not taken the proper time to get to know someone then we have to deal with serious issues, we will inevitably fall short of the mark.

Then, after years of being together, one day somebody is going to wake up and say, "I don't want to do this anymore." This is why the divorce rate is where it is today. This is why we see people stay in relationships for extended periods without any forward progress. This is why people marry those who are obviously wrong for them. And last but not least, this is why we continue to have failed relationship after failed relationship, never knowing why, how, or when everything went wrong.

Have you ever been on autopilot? Have you ever been involved in something that in retrospect was toxic for you, but at the time you had no way to avoid it or resist it? Have you ever met someone, become intimate and exclusive, and then broken up in such a short time that you were left wondering what even happened? Have you ever been with somebody four, five, or even six years, only to end up breaking up? Do you know someone who's been married for fifteen years and one day they're divorced and counting their losses?

It leaves you wondering how something like that could happen. Autopilot love has no time restrictions or boundaries. It happens regardless of race, age, or sexual preference. Autopilot love is simply unforgiving, and if you aren't careful, it is something that you will never be able to overcome for the simple fact that you aren't aware of it. If you ask the average person why their relationship failed, they will either blame the other person, blame their job, their circumstances, or the fact that they just weren't ready. What they won't do is admit that they weren't aware of their triggers or that they didn't love that person, but rather the idea of them, and before they knew it, they were flying the friendly skies of autopilot love without being equipped to land safely once it was time to take control.

Now that we've uncovered a lot of the pitfalls that we fall victim to so often, we're able to examine what we need to do to move forward and begin to experience relationship success. It's not enough to move forward with bustling optimism before we've taken the time to look at the clues we can uncover from the failures we've experienced in the past.

At this point, we should be operating from a completely different mindset than before, and that's when real change occurs. While this mindset shift is a great start, it's also important to understand the environments in which autopilot love thrives – the dating world and our society's views on love and marriage.

Questions to ask yourself:

1. Have I ever experienced autopilot love?
2. Am I currently on autopilot?
3. What are the triggers that I need to be aware of?

5

The Dating Conundrum

In your self-reflection after a fall or after taking time to think about the questions in the previous chapter, you might have asked yourself: What can I do to avoid the trap of autopilot love? How can I be more aware of myself and those around me? Will I ever be able to find someone?

In order to find these answers, you must understand two things and understand them well — dating in the twenty-first century creates bad relationships and people need to qualify for your time.

The Way We Date Is Broken

Dating in the twenty-first century is rough. Let's just be honest about it. If you are single in today's dating climate, then you are up against potholes, obstacles, and plot twists that past generations simply didn't have to deal with, and at the very least, a lot more of what they did have to deal with.

The information age has made it so that you can have instant access to almost anyone on the planet with an internet connection, and it gives you the ability to use that access for the highest level of good, the highest level of bad, and every iteration in between. You can be single and choose to meet people the old-fashioned way; you can hop on dating sites and try your luck there; or you can play the numbers game and slide into as many DMs as possible or comment on every story, status update, picture, YouTube video, Snap, vlog, and/or podcast until you get a proverbial hit.

If you combine this with the fact that we're right in the middle of a "want it right now" society, then it becomes increasingly difficult to resist the temptation to feel like we are missing out on something if we're not in a perpetual state of playing the field or going on tons of dates (i.e., dating).

The result of today's dating climate is that we have people agreeing to meet other people without having a complete picture of who they are, and for whatever reason, we have bought into the idea that we'll just give as many people a test run as we possibly can until we hit the jackpot. If she's fine as hell, then she gets a chance, and if he's handsome and somewhat successful, then he could be bae.

Because we are bombarded with so many options and so many ways to connect, we go for quantity instead of quality. What happens is we end up having dated this guy for eighteen months, living with this other girl for two years, and at the culmination of all our dating efforts, we're often left picking up the pieces and starting over from square one with months and years of our lives stolen from us and no way of getting them back. We make a quick promise to ourselves never to repeat the cycle, and then when we think we're ready, we take the plunge right back into the same ocean of people we were in before. Same bait, same boat, same mindset.

Modern dating restricts you from learning who someone is. Why? Because dating limits your ability to get to know someone on a genuine level. First, dating does *not* give you an accurate representation of who someone is. It does not and it absolutely cannot. Any guy can give plasma for a few weeks, get a haircut from their roommate, and buy a blazer at a discount store to make a good first impression. Any girl can get her hair done, have her roommate do her makeup, and put on her best pair of heels to make a good impression. Anyone can put on a facade to get what they want, but it doesn't mean that's who they really are.

How many times have you gone on a date only to find out the person you met at the dinner table wasn't the same person behind closed doors? How many times have you been wined and dined only to discover someone couldn't be more wrong for you? A buddy of mine once told me that he was really into a young lady after going on a date or two with her. The conversation was incredible, the vibe was delightful, and all the green lights were there.

One day he was at work and his new acquaintance offered to pick him up for a quick lunch meetup together. To his dismay, when he met her in the parking lot, he discovered that her car was an absolute dump. Double cheeseburger wrappers, empty Gatorade bottles, papers, and a smell that would make anyone run for the hills. Needless to say, after their lunch, he decided to end their relationship as politely as possible. Long story short, dating does not prove anything other than the fact that someone can look nice for one evening out or for a few weeks.

Second, people typically don't discuss personal and/or sensitive topics while on dates or while dating. We engage in weeks and months of surface talk. Why? Because when you are dating, your focus typically isn't on getting to know someone on a deep, tangible level. Your focus is on trying to demonstrate why they should choose you. In layman's terms, you're trying to impress them.

In the social sphere, financial space, and the bedroom, dating is just an audition. When things go south, we typically just walk out and see who else is having a casting call. And when you're trying to impress someone, all of the sensitive topics go out the window for fear of being judged or rejected based on your past. This is how people can date for three years and not know whether the other person wants kids or not.

When your attempt to get to know someone is filtered through the lens of dating, it skews your perception of things they say and do and causes you to either ignore signs that are right in front of you or create problems that aren't there. Combined with autopilot love, we end up focusing on the wrong things. If you're not careful, trying to discover your partner through the lens of dating can be the exact thing that is preventing you from finding the one that is waiting for you.

Right now, there are some people who not only know who their spouse is, but have met them, interacted with them, and even hung out with them on several occasions. But because they are so quick to jump from relationship to relationship without the proper factfinding and because they only consider someone relationship material *after* they've gone on a date with them, they continue to postpone, sabotage, and derail the chance to connect with their perfect match.

Instead of "looking for love," we can instead focus on looking for compatibility, true friendship, and genuine connection. Then we can begin to take an accurate survey of our relationship landscape and discover who would be best for us in the long run.

Instead of looking for relationships, we need to switch gears and begin looking for the compatibility on which the relationship will be based.

"You're not supposed to date someone to find out if they're right for you. You're supposed to find out if someone is right for you so that you can date them."

But what does this say about our culture that we don't take the time to know others before we get serious? What does it say about our society when dating has become something that means nothing? Is there any chance that people will slow down when everything around us is begging us to speed up? To take risks? To have it now? How did we get to a place where people continue to get their hearts broken over and over but never take time to look at *why* and only focus on who's to blame? How do we solve the dating conundrum? More importantly, can it be solved? And how?

The answer is simple: let people qualify first.

Let People Qualify First

Too often we are quick to give the best parts of ourselves to others before they have demonstrated that they deserve it. We will spend money on other people, wine and dine them, cook and clean for them, and even give them sexual access to us. We'll go out of our way to see them whenever they're free. We'll take days off of work and inconvenience ourselves for others. We'll even move in with people who simply *do not deserve it*. It leaves us bitter, resentful, drained, and enraged.

But more than anything, it leaves us questioning whether or not we are good enough, or whether we'll ever find someone who values what we bring to the table. We continuously make the mistake and suffer the injury. And after we think we've healed from our missteps, we jump right back out there and do the same thing, in the same way, hoping that this time will be different.

People need to qualify to be in your life. At all levels and in all capacities, but especially in relationships. Whether it be friendships or marriage, people need to demonstrate over time and in many capacities that they are in your life to give more than they take away. When you approach a new relationship with your hands open and haven't confirmed who you're opening your hand to, it's no wonder people keep getting taken advantage of and keep having trouble finding someone right for them. Qualify your connections and you'll find that it's much easier to choose when to take the next step into something more serious. Look for things that indicate character, like integrity, honesty, and authenticity, instead of focusing on superficial traits like looks, common interests, and hobbies you may have in common. This will go a *long* way.

To avoid this, we have to take control of our relationships from the *beginning*. *Not* the middle and definitely not the end. That means you must first value your time, money, energy, and effort enough to *not* give it away.

When my then-girlfriend (now wife) and I went out on one of our first dates, she ordered the lobster tail. It was one of the priciest things on the menu. Now, I wasn't upset that she chose it, but later that evening I had an epiphany. The reason I was so willing to take her out and buy the lobster tail is that she deserved it. At this point in our relationship, she had demonstrated and communicated her worth to me in several different ways, and as my girlfriend, I had no problem doing that for her.

But had that been some random chick I had just met a week or two prior? Had that been some "potential" I was testing the waters with, I would have regretted buying that lobster tail and wasting my money on something that was going nowhere.

Some might say that's just the cost of doing business. Don't hate the player, hate the game. The thing is that there's another game you can play, a game that allows you to not have to use your resources in an attempt to turn nothing into something. It's called being friends first. It's called getting to know someone so much so that once the time comes to paint the town red, you can move forward with confidence and not a wishful mentality. You can move forward knowing that your energy won't be wasted. A few phone conversations and a pretty smile should not be enough for someone to qualify for your time, but becoming friends first should.

How many times have you heard the story of the woman who moved in with a guy, cooked his meals and washed his clothes, memorized every position in the Kama Sutra, and never received the same treatment in return? Or he broke up with her? Or he cheated? Or he stayed with her for ten years and never proposed? How many times have we heard about the guy who maxes out his credit cards to wine and dine a lady, takes her on trips, and makes sure all of her needs are met, only to have her nag and complain that he doesn't do more? Or she starts spending his money recklessly instead of showing gratitude? Or she plays the victim when he asks if she can do more for him?

It happens *all* the time and it's the worst situation to be in. You are under no obligation to pay for anything, dress a certain way, or give anyone anything that they haven't *earned* from you. The keyword here is "earned." And no, it's not about being stingy, feeling like you have power over someone, feeling like you're better than someone, or going tit for tat. It's about valuing what you have enough to *not* give it away on a whim. It's interesting because we'll be pickier with who we allow into our social circles than who we allow into our bedroom. We'll set up strict barriers and protocols in the public sphere but open our wallets without a second thought. A lot of us have it completely backward.

More specifically, I think that most of us treat refraining from giving sexual access to someone as a way of demonstrating patience, but for some reason, we act as if that's the only area that should be off-limits to most people, at least right away. But usually, most other parts of us are given freely. Understand, however, that scarcity should apply to more than just sex. Understand that *anything* you have to give is valuable. Your time, your attention, your conversation, and your resources are all things that need to be safeguarded. Period.

We play a dangerous and costly game when we are so willing and oftentimes eager to impress others that we give before we are sure they should even receive. If anyone can have it, then it's not very valuable, and if anyone can have *you* after a few dates or a little bit of liquid courage, then you're communicating that you aren't thinking long term, even though you tell yourself that you are.

"If anyone can have it, then it's not very valuable."

When we finally settle down and say "I do," what happens next? Well, about 50% of people realize that they chose the wrong person and for one reason or another, they get divorced. What this tells us is that in the current climate of dating, the odds of your relationship going the distance are the same as a coin toss. Think about that for a second. In today's dating scene, the odds of you and the person sleeping next to you tonight going the distance are about as good as you calling heads or tails.

That is downright *scary!* To know that your odds of success are average at best should be reason enough for you to stop and take a moment to accept the truth of how relationships aren't something you can just slide into because of superficial reasons and surface talk. You need to dig deep early and often and press into this until you get it right. Remember what I said earlier. It's easy to get it. But it's hard as hell to get it right!

This means that when the world is telling you to go on three dates before you let him have some or wait ninety days to get intimate, or buy a ring after eighteen months of dating, that you go against the grain and put on your detective hat until further notice. One quote I heard a few years ago about marketing rings true in relationships as well: "Pay attention to what everyone else is doing, and then do the exact opposite." Best. Advice. Ever.

"Pay attention to what everyone else is doing and then do the exact opposite."

If we see that relationships are failing at an all-time high, then we know that whatever seems to be the norm is something that is not effective, and we know that logically, it's in our best interest to do something else. I don't know about you, but leaving your most intimate relationships up to a coin toss is not something that sounds appealing.

Hit the pause button. Wherever you are or whoever you are, take a moment to stop. Put your life on "do not disturb" for a few days, weeks, or months, and really think about what your relationship experience has been up until this point. Look for any trends, good or bad, and do something you probably have never done. Ask yourself *why* dating doesn't work for you.

Questions to ask yourself:

1. Has dating worked for me? Why or why not?
2. When was the last time I examined why I can't seem to find someone?
3. Have I ever really qualified someone before dating them?
4. What adjustments can I make in this area of my life?
5. Have I ever examined the benefits of not dating and focusing on building friendships?

6

Love Is Scary

What is love? Seriously, what is it? Is it an act or a feeling or a gesture or an emotion? Can you love someone unconditionally? Can you fall out of love and if so, does that mean you weren't ever really in love to begin with? Why does love hurt? This is such a broad idea to tackle because if you ask a thousand people what love is, you might get a thousand different answers, ranging from casual to more serious.

If we watch four episodes of a new show and it captivates us for one reason or another, we're quick to slide over to social media and proclaim that we love it. If we find a new ice cream flavor at the local market that we've never tried and it turns out to be amazing, we might say we love it and automatically label it as our new favorite.

Are you sensing a pattern here? We tend to use the word love so often in our daily lives that when we mention it in the sphere of personal relationships, it just feels natural to say. Meet someone and they are charismatic or rich or great in bed, and we will sling the word love around at the drop of a dime.

If that weren't shocking enough, if you ask someone why they "love" someone they just met three months ago, they wouldn't even be able to tell you why (more on this later). They wouldn't even be able to articulate what they feel, but they would be certain that it was love.

If you asked someone to name four reasons why they love the person they've been dating for a few months, they would say things like they're supportive, they're charming and thoughtful, or they have a great sense of humor. Or they might flat-out say, "I don't know, but there's something about them I just love." And based solely on this sense of love, we will dive headfirst into something that we have no idea about. Don't agree? The next time one of your friends gets into a relationship, ask them, "What do you like about them?" And then sit back and listen to what they say.

If we are in love (autopilot or otherwise), love can have no definition but every definition depending on the circumstance. But as we grow, learn, and experience life, one thing we can say with absolute certainty is that love is scary. Love is scary for a variety of reasons, but the one that stands out like a whale on the beach is the fact that love is unpredictable. Something that we give seemingly unlimited power to is something we often can't control. We've heard stories of people murdering for love, falling into deep, deep depressions because of love, achieving their greatest accomplishments because of love, and much, much more.

Love can even extend beyond people and apply to things, animals, ideas, concepts, movements, and beliefs. It would seem that we have the capacity to love just about anything, and, given the right circumstances, we'll do and endure almost anything in the name of love.

Because humans are naturally wired for survival, whenever we find something or someone we connect with, our survival mechanism kicks in when we are drawn to those things. So even if we can't express with words why we love someone, all we know is that we *feel* it, and what we feel has to be valid, right? Well, yes and no. If you feel something, then those feelings are valid to a certain degree — but that does *not* mean that you must act on those feelings no matter what.

Think of it this way. If you saw a burning building at the end of the block and you heard the cries of someone on the eleventh floor, your first instinct might be to run in without a second thought. However, just because you feel you can save the neighbor does not mean that reality will line up in the same way. It may be hard to accept the fact that what you feel isn't what you should do, but if you ignore logic when it comes to matters of the heart, then you can put yourself in harm's way, just as if you were running into a burning building.

I know that some of us are ready for love and have been for a while, but the thought of missing out on love cannot overpower the desire to make better decisions when it comes to relationships. If we allow love to take the driver's seat above all else, there's always a chance that we'll fall victim to it instead of being saved by it.

Sex Is Powerful

Just like love, sexual feelings can sometimes lead us to take actions that don't align with what we should do in reality. We all know the pitfalls of having sex too early in relationships. *All* of us. We know that when we have sex, it clouds our judgment, prohibits us from seeing obvious red flags, and makes us give people the benefit of the doubt with the quickness. Sex will blind you to who someone is and has caused more failed relationships than anything else. Sex typically is an automatic response to feelings of fondness that we have towards others. We tend to believe that having sex with someone is how we display that we like them and that it's the best way to do so.

Crazy enough, many people will think that you don't like them if you don't show any signs of wanting to sleep with them after a certain number of dates or a certain amount of time spent getting to know them. Imagine that. And when asked what they think, many will answer, "They never made a move, so I didn't think they were into me." Yet, in knowing the dangers of having sex before developing a true friendship with someone, we continue to repeat toxic sexual behavior, never once taking inventory of why we continue to choose the wrong person, give our bodies away, and get our hearts broken.

We're not going to spend too much time on the topic of sex because it's not necessary. The only thing that people need to understand is that the earlier you have sex, the more trouble you are exposing yourself to. Why? Even though we all like to tell ourselves that we can shuffle people in and out of our bedrooms without forming attachments, that simply isn't true. Sex is designed to allow two people to form a connection with one another. That's literally what it's meant for beyond the natural function of procreation. So when you jump in the bed with someone, you are creating emotional, physical, and mental ties to the person whether you want to admit it or not. Can you see how that might not work out in your best interest if your bed buddy is someone who is not good for you?

There are a good majority of people who value sexual compatibility above all other things. If the person they're with can't please them on a certain level, then they will throw the possibility of being with that person out the window entirely. Likewise, if they come across someone that performs well in that area, they are more willing to put up with major deficiencies in other areas for the sake of a great time between the sheets.

Sadly, the same way we soak up societal behaviors such as how we talk, how we should dress, or how we should cut our hair is the same way we soak up relationship behaviors like what qualities to prioritize, if we should or shouldn't move in together, and how quickly we should become intimate. It happens so subtly and so gradually that we never notice. This means we eventually come to a place where we simply accept a lot of behaviors that happen in relationships as just the way it's supposed to be. It's why we see people having sex on the first date or why people stay in unfulfilling relationships for years on end. Sex has almost become a measuring stick (no pun intended) for how good a relationship could be or a pacifier for relationships that need to end.

I guess you could look at it as a "get out of jail free" card of sorts. Something you can use in virtually any relationship situation to justify toxic behaviors, to cure loneliness, to express your affection towards someone, or to quickly see if someone could be right for you. We've essentially turned an intimate, personal, and sacred act into just another thing to do, not realizing that it's precisely the behavior that is causing us to miss the mark.

I would strongly suggest that you reserve your body only for those who are worthy of it. I know that we all have needs, and those needs can cloud our judgment worse than almost anything else, but man or woman, not everyone deserves to enjoy the experience of being with you in that capacity. And when we give that part of us away over and over again, we diminish its value both to ourselves and others.

Understand the power of sex and understand that when it comes to finding "the one," you're better off exercising patience. This communicates that they should value what you have to offer because you value it first. There should be no ninety-day rule. There should be no three-date rule. There should be no rule at all. The only thing that matters is knowing before the fact that the person in bed with you is someone that you have a true connection with when you're not in the bed with them. And like we said before, getting to know someone on a deep, personal level takes *way* more time than most of us are willing to spend.

Not the Cause, the Effect

Love is not an action, nor is it a feeling in and of itself. Love is the byproduct of our perceived level of connection. Hear me out. Whatever your measuring stick is for connection or compatibility, if you feel like you've found the person who meets or exceeds your standard for what a relationship should look like, then as a result, you will feel feelings of love and fondness.

We can neither fall in love nor out of love. We can only have our needs met or not met, and love will follow as a result. What happens is that when you fall out of love, you're just realizing that the person you are or were with doesn't meet your standard of compatibility like you once thought they did. So if you keep falling in love over and over with the wrong people, it's not because you're gullible or naive. It's because your metric for compatibility is not conducive to long-lasting success.

Put another way, the things you're looking for in a mate

need to change. That's it. If we would take a moment to sit down and update our standard of what it means to find that special someone, then we would find that it would cure a lot of the problems that we encounter in relationships, especially marriage. Just like love and sex, our society has downplayed just what marriage is – one of the most serious decisions you can make in life.

Questions to ask yourself:

1. Has love driven me to make rash or unwise decisions?
2. When I rush into a physical relationship, does it ever work out?
3. What can I learn from the mistakes I've made in the areas of love and sex?

7

Marriage Is Serious

Marriage is one of the most beautiful things this life has to offer, but in the same token, it can be detrimental when not treated that way. The reason we need to discuss marriage is that it's not just a continuation of being someone's boyfriend or girlfriend. You don't just slap a signature on a marriage license, throw a big party, and carry on. It's serious.

When people don't understand the seriousness of what they are getting into, then they end up getting hurt. They find themselves caught up in the whirlwind of buying a dress and planning a wedding and wearing a ring. They focus on everything except getting to know their future spouse on a deep, vulnerable, transparent level. When the rubber meets the road and God forbid things don't work out, we inevitably end up blaming the other person for simply being who they were all along: somebody we were never supposed to be with in the first place. When it comes to marriage, you need to be crystal clear on what it is that is waiting for you. We need to dedicate ourselves to the idea that choosing the right one is worth the wait.

There are countless magazines, blogs, websites, and shows dedicated to showing the beauty and importance of the big day, but when it comes to showcasing the beauty and importance of cultivating a lifelong connection, there's no competition. With the exception of a few good relationship books, the majority of popular media is about the glam of the wedding day and not the importance of the bond between the newlyweds. When was the last time you saw a show called "Strong, Healthy Marriage"?

Marriage is the single biggest commitment you can make in life. It's two people who are vowing to dedicate their lives in every single capacity to one another for the rest of their lives. Marriage is meant to be a *permanent* union that binds two souls in a way that nothing else can. Too often we see people who get married only to discover the painful reality of their incorrect choice. The choice to make a forever commitment to a temporary someone.

Our society, as it's presently constructed, has led people to believe that if you have any level of chemistry with someone, if the sex is good, and if you have a few things in common, there must be something about this person that's worth exploring on a deeper level. Our society has people believing that marriage isn't a serious, intentional decision that can cripple you if you choose wrong, even though it is.

Part of the problem is that many of us have *never* been taught the seriousness of marriage and don't understand what we're doing when we say those vows. Marriage has been romanticized so much that we focus mostly on the wedding day and not the forty or fifty years of effort and work that are waiting for the two of you on the backend.

What Is Marriage?

Marriage is meant to be an eternal commitment made by two people that prioritize helping each other to achieve their ultimate purpose during their time on this earth. It is an extremely intimate, powerful, intentional, and deliberate act of faith that requires your dedication, honesty, vulnerability, and a desire to do everything in your power to make your partner better. When you get married, words like *I, me,* and *my* disappear and are replaced with words like *us, we,* and *our.* Marriage is the ultimate gesture of love and is meant to last forever. Two people committing their all to one person for the rest of their lives.

When you choose a mate, it should be someone who you know is going to make you better, hold you accountable, speak life into you, motivate you, correct you, and be your hiding place in hard times. Your spouse is a direct reflection of you and represents the legacy you will leave behind on this earth. You should be proud to have your spouse by your side, and you should hold them in the highest esteem regardless of circumstance or situation. Your spouse should make you a better person.

Marriage is a declaration to the world that you have found the one person worthy of all that you have to give, both now and forever. You do not marry someone because you love them. You marry someone because their existence contributes to your life in a positive, tangible, ongoing way that adds much more than it takes away, and from that, love will undoubtedly be present.

Marriage is not to be dealt with lightly and not entered into hastily or without serious consideration. Marriage communicates both directly and indirectly that you have found the only person worthy of a lifelong commitment, and marrying the right person will feel like the best decision in the entire world, not because of feeling, but because of knowing. Marriage constitutes a daily choice to make your spouse the most important person in your entire life. Marriage is not a wedding day, but a choice to grow together with one person and give up selfish desires for the benefit of the union.

It's about creating a legacy that your family can look up to and your kids can be proud of. Marriage is not being someone's boyfriend forever. Marriage is not playing house. Marriage is not two people living under one roof, operating independently of one another. Marriage is overflowing with intimacy, joy, growth, struggle, work, and compromise. Marriage is *not* easy. Marriage will expose every single one of your flaws and force both of you to confront them and grow through them one by one. Marriage is serious.

Don't Become Another Statistic

We've all witnessed the rise of divorce in society and have every reason to believe that it won't be slowing down anytime soon. We see people hopping in and out of marriages as if marriage is some fad. Treating marriage like it's the "in" thing to do right now, using it as a chance to one-up friends or get clout on social media. It's an expensive way to show off — the average cost of a wedding in the United States in 2019 was $33,900, not including the honeymoon. And studies have shown that the more expensive the wedding and the rings, the more likely the union will end in divorce.

What people don't realize is that when you get married, you are marrying the "everyday" version of someone. The version that has road rage and anger issues. The version that has insecurities and trust issues. The version that has bad hygiene and hoarding issues. The version that no one in the public eye will ever see. That is the version that you're going to be getting after the cake is eaten and the bouquet gets tossed.

When we accelerate the dating process, fail to become friends first, and approach marriage like a game, we fall in love with the idealized version of someone and end up disappointed on the other side of the wedding when we find out who they are. That's why getting to know someone is so critical. If you go on a few dates, have sex, and participate in a whirlwind romance where marriage seems like a logical conclusion, you are playing Russian roulette. Taking the time to be someone's friend gives you the true story behind who someone is and allows you to make a decision based on facts and not feelings.

Let's talk about divorce. What we always hear is that the number one reason why couples get divorced is due to arguments and disagreements over money in some form or fashion. This reasoning, while still factual, is incorrect. Money fights are not the *real* reason behind why so many marriages fail, but rather just another symptom. The real reason the odds of a marriage going the distance are about as good as a coin toss is that people are marrying people that they simply do not know. Period.

People are making lifelong commitments to someone that they have never really gotten to know, and seeing as how we live in a world that runs on money, it makes sense why that would be one of the more common pain points that end up dividing people. But it's not the root cause. It's not money that's the issue. It's not knowing how your spouse handles money that is the problem.

Our society has pushed the idea that if you don't like it, there's a simple exit strategy that will allow you to walk away unscathed.

The funny thing is that walking away unscathed from marriage simply isn't possible. When you get a divorce, there will be a serious price to pay —financially, emotionally, psychologically, and the list goes on.

Just like dating and love, people don't take marriage nearly as seriously as they should. But now that you see our culture's views on relationships for what they are, you can turn within to see how you've played a role in your love life up until now. Let's take another dive within.

Questions to ask yourself:

1. Do I understand what marriage is truly about?
2. Do I consider divorce an option? Why or why not?
3. Have I had the chance to witness what a healthy marriage looks like?
4. How have I prepared myself for the effort it takes to make a marriage work?

8

You Were Wrong

Now that you can see the pitfalls of modern dating and relationships, you might want to get right to the details of approaching relationships as friends first. But before you can begin to explore the benefits, you need to take a moment to be honest about where you are. Part of that honesty is admitting to yourself that you don't know how to choose the right person to be with.

Whether it be from a lack of patience on your part or just flat-out negligence, there's something you are or are not doing that is causing you to slide into a relationship and slide out just as easily, injuries in tow. It might even be because no one ever equipped you with the knowledge of how to choose. The point is that if you're honest, you'll see all of what you've gone through in relationships could have been avoided if you had gone about choosing your partners better.

Repeat after me...

I don't know how to choose a partner and I must learn how.

It's *very* important for you to be honest and objective when it comes to finding someone. It doesn't mean applying robotic, emotionless logic, but it means you need to be an adult about the situation. Part of finding someone is being able to look at the information in front of you and provide an unbiased assessment of what's happening as it's happening.

Now, let's explore some of the reasons why you continue to choose the wrong person and end up on autopilot. Most relationship blunders fall into one or more of five different areas.

1. You weren't patient enough.

This one is simple. You just didn't wait long enough before saying "let's do this." Either because of desperation or sheer impatience, you met someone and before you knew it, you were calling them your boo and introducing them to your parents and closest friends. You may have slipped up and used the L-word too. You didn't take the necessary time to qualify them. There are some people right now who, if they had waited for as little as a few extra weeks to spend time getting to know the other person, would have *never* become exclusive and could have avoided a world of heartbreak. This one is easy. You chose wrong because you chose too quickly. Slow down, playa.

2. You didn't ask questions.

We always ask questions. It's a natural part of meeting someone new. How old are you? Where were you born? What's your favorite color? But when it comes to inviting another human into our life, a lot of us simply need to ask more questions — and much better questions. What's your idea of a healthy marriage? How do you handle conflict? Does parental success harm children?

I'm not sure if it's because we simply don't know what constitutes a better question or if we are afraid to disqualify someone because we've already convinced ourselves we like them so much. If we don't ask these questions early and often to get to the core of who is sitting across the table from us, then how can we ever be confident in saying that they deserve to be with us? How can we avoid pitfalls that will eventually come up?

Additionally, we live in a world where we worry so much about being politically correct that sometimes we'll actively choose *not* to ask the important questions that we know we should for fear of running the other person off or making them feel uncomfortable. But again, this isn't about them. It's about making sure that you know who you're talking to before things get serious on any level. It's a way of safeguarding your life from unnecessary and, more importantly, avoidable situations, and all it takes is a few more questions.

You chose wrong because you didn't ask the proper questions, so you didn't get the proper answers until it was too late.

3. You ignored the red flags.

This is the one that trips us up the most. Even if we are patient and ask the right questions when faced with the red flags that should make us pause, a lot of us still make the wrong choice. We are still prone to overlook the flaws of others for several reasons, which can include the amount of money they make per year, the car they drive, how physically attractive they are, how amazingly they perform in bed, how charismatic they are, their accent, or how you two have very similar interests.

When we connect with someone and there's chemistry, we become so enamored with what we like about them that we make excuses for and flat-out ignore the things we know deep down are not good for us. We will date, have sex with, and even move in with people who are toxic and harmful to what we're trying to achieve because we have made up in our minds that they are who we need to be with. You enjoy the sex but ignore the laziness, or you fall in love with the physical appearance but you tell yourself you can deal with the control issues and clinginess.

Think of it this way: if you were hanging out of the side of a plane about to skydive, and right as you were about to take that leap, you noticed that a clamp on your parachute was bent, damaged, and looked unsafe, would you jump? If you noticed that the cord you pull to deploy your chute was tattered and looked like it could rip if you pulled it too hard, would you jump? Hell no!

Now imagine you ignore the red flags and jump despite seeing them. For a short while, you'd have the time of your life. The thrill of free falling, the view from above. The adrenaline rush. It would be epic. But then, when it counts the most, you'd try to open up your parachute and there would be no guarantee it would open correctly. There would be no guarantee it would open *at all*.

And that's where you would find yourself. In need of help, in need of support. Feeling helpless and afraid. Instantly regretting your decision to jump and having no idea what will happen when you hit the bottom. Lastly, you would remember the fact that you saw the warning signs and jumped anyway. You'd ask yourself over and over, "Why did I put myself in harm's way on purpose?"

A classic example that I have seen is people who desire to be married and will still choose to engage in a committed relationship with someone who is on the fence about marriage, isn't ready, or has not expressed a sincere desire to be married soon. After years and years of waiting and hoping that they will change their mind or see the light, the relationship either falls apart or the hopeful partner ends up waiting *way* beyond the timeframe they had hoped. Either way, the cards were played in the very beginning, and because these signs were ignored or simply disregarded, people will unnecessarily add years to their ex-year count.

When you choose wrong, you are gambling with your well-being. It's been stated once already, but you need to understand that choosing the wrong person can destroy your life. The real question is: would you rather deal with the pain and the emotional consequences of choosing wrong, or would you rather remain single and deal with the temporary discomfort (if you want to call it that) of operating solo until you find the person that you're most compatible with? I know it's easier said than done, but when you become serious about finding a life partner, you need to approach any new relationship with as many facts as possible, a sobering resolve to get it right, and the confidence to walk away if that's what needs to be done.

You chose wrong because you ignored the red flags and it almost cost you everything.

4. You got desperate.

After you've been single for several years or after you've gotten invited to your seventh wedding this year, you got desperate and just said yes to the first person that came along and made you feel good. Maybe they were a rebound thing, or maybe they were the most attractive person you've ever met. You didn't ask any questions, you didn't wait, and you didn't even give yourself enough time to discover any red flags, let alone use them to make an informed decision. You simply dove in with no regard to your safety or well-being and decided to figure it out along the way. *Bad* move.

When you reach the point of desperation, you are in dangerous territory. Desperation can make you irrational, indifferent, too forgiving, overzealous, and flat-out naive about something life-altering. Being desperate is how you stay in toxic relationships and it's how you stay in relationships that you *know* are never going to serve you in the way you need to be happy, peaceful, and content. When you get desperate, you can't live your best life. When it's all said and done, you chose wrong because you got desperate, and desperation will make you do anything.

5. You didn't take things seriously.

Not taking a relationship seriously happens in a handful of ways. On one hand, we're starting to see more and more people who are trying to have the best of both worlds by being in an "open" relationship. A relationship where they are kind of exclusive but not exclusive 100%. They can still enjoy the benefits of a serious relationship, but don't have to have an official title.

A relationship where they don't have to call each other every day, but they can't go without calling each other for more than several days. A relationship where they go on dates, but sometimes he pays and sometimes she pays. A relationship where they can have sex with other people, but they have to tell the other person about it first. A relationship where everything is ambiguous and vague and unclear and not "serious." This is where we have two people actively trying to enjoy the benefits of exclusivity while still having the freedoms of being single.

Not taking a relationship seriously can then manifest itself in the form of making promises you can't keep, being unfaithful, never setting any expectations or boundaries, and even allowing the person you're with to take advantage of you. It's a situation where two people say yes to everything in the name of not wanting to put a label on anything. Not wanting to force the issue or make the other person uncomfortable: Do you want to see other people? Yes! Is it ok if I stay out until 3:00 a.m. and not let you know where I am? Yes! I lost my job and have not actively looked for one in six months, can I borrow $600? Yes.

Additionally, not taking it seriously can look like falling into a head-over-heels entanglement and throwing all bit of caution to the wind. Giving up your time, resources, body, and emotions only to be met with the harsh reality waiting for you on the other side of separation. In this case, you chose wrong because you didn't understand that a committed relationship with another person is much more than just "I love you" and "It's us against the world."

No matter your age or the details of how you met, *every* relationship is serious and has the potential to change your life for better or for worse. That being said, you must approach it with a healthy balance of rhyme (love) and reason (logic).

Regardless of the how or why, you chose wrong because you

convinced yourself that it wasn't as serious as it was, either because you were trying to guard your heart against being broken, you told yourself that you wouldn't get attached this time, or you jumped in with both eyes closed.

When you don't take relationships seriously, what you're saying is that you don't want the full responsibility of a relationship, but you do want all the benefits. This is dangerous territory because at some point, emotions will surface, and at that point, a decision will need to be made as to what the plan will be moving forward. That's just the way people are. For a moment it's all fun and games, but when time passes and you form connections, not being serious won't be enough. At some point, someone is going to be emotionally invested, and having fun won't be an option anymore. Unfortunately, that's when people walk away from the situation and use the fact that they've never been "serious" as a scapegoat, absolving them of all responsibility. In the end, you chose wrong because you didn't take things seriously and you got burned, or you burned someone else.

Choosing wrong is not a fun experience, and oftentimes we feel as though we've done our due diligence only to find out we couldn't have been more incorrect. I've been there, and I know how painful it can be. But if we make sure that we're patient, that we ask the right questions, that we pay close attention to the red flags, and we don't get desperate or lackadaisical, we'll have a much better chance of finding the person that we'll be with long term.

When we ignore these protocols, we set ourselves up for failure before we even begin. All things considered, if we do everything we can to choose right, then we'll choose wrong much less often. It's not enough to want to get it — we have to be focused on getting it right.

Questions to ask yourself:

1. What red flags have I avoided or ignored that ended in a failed relationship?
2. Are there certain red flags that I have a habit of avoiding or ignoring?
3. What questions can I ask to uncover red flags sooner?
4. Why have my relationships failed in the past?

9

The Ex-Years

One of the most tangible representations of why being friends first is important is an idea I like to refer to as the "ex years." Your ex years are simply the number of years of your life that you've spent giving the best parts of yourself to someone who wasn't supposed to have them. It's a concrete example of how serious choosing correctly really is and also how easily we can waste time when we repeatedly make the wrong decisions.

Add up the total number of years across all of your failed relationships and you'll arrive at your particular number. For example, say you were with your first ex for two years, your second ex for four years, and your most recent ex for one year. Your number would be seven. This number is a graphic representation of how much time you could have spent getting to know people on a deeper level rather than committing yourself to someone you were never supposed to be with in the first place.

I have close to ten ex years, a combination of three serious relationships as well as a few summer flings and short periods of dating. What that means is that for almost a decade of my life, I dedicated my time, money, consideration, energy, attention, patience, and love to someone who was never supposed to have those things or who I was wrong for. Almost a decade of my life spent exclusively either with someone who didn't qualify or who I didn't qualify for and should have never made it through the proverbial front door. Almost a third of my life that I can't get back.

The 'ex-years'

Relationship #1 - 0.5
Relationship #2 - 3.5
Relationship #3 - 5.5

Total Ex Years = 9.5

In relationships, it is important to learn from our mistakes and use those lessons to shape the way we approach relationships in the future, but when you look at the number of years that it takes most people to finally settle down, there's one simple question that surfaces. Is there a better way? Should it take someone five, ten, or even twenty ex years to finally understand what it means to choose the right person? Does it take that long to finally realize what we want in a mate? I think that answer is a solid no. There is a better way, and it shouldn't take someone a decade of shortcomings to finally win at relationships.

The lessons learned from past relationships are invaluable, but a lot of those lessons can be learned without the sacrifice of your best years in exchange. For some, they wouldn't have met Mr. Right if Mr. Wrong hadn't been right on time. But how about we avoid Mr. Wrong altogether and simply wait patiently for Mr. Right? Wouldn't it make more sense to prioritize the preservation of your best for the person who deserves it most instead of participating in what, for most people, ends up being a reactionary, surface-level attempt at finding the right person? Doesn't it make more sense to be friends first and rely on what we know and can verify instead of what we feel? I propose that dating someone is not the only way to find out who someone is. And more than anything, your number should be a stark reminder of why.

What's your number? How many years of your life have you spent giving your best to someone who wasn't meant to experience it? How much of your time, your money, and your attention have you given exclusively to someone who wasted it with reckless abandon? What could you have done with all of those years you can't get back?

A better question you should ask yourself is: how many friendships could you have cultivated in those years? How much more of yourself could you have discovered? How much could you have grown as a person during that period when your time and attention were dominated by just one person? How many people could you have met and connections could you have fostered if you weren't preoccupied with a relationship that was headed nowhere? How would things be different if you were friends for all those years instead of wasting time? What would you do if you could get those ex years back?

For many, your ex years will serve as a serious pain point. An unforgiving reminder of just how wrong you were or continue to be. Your ex years will haunt you and prevent you from moving forward with confidence because of the fear that the past will only serve as the most likely outcome in the future. Depending on where you are in life, you may even feel as though there's no use in trying to get it right or that you should throw in the towel and either be single forever or throw caution to the wind and let the chips fall where they may.

It's at this critical point in your life, however, that you should feel empowered. Pain can be a good thing if you use it as a catalyst for change and as a reference point for the future. Your ex years don't define you, but they should enlighten you.

Knowing that whatever you've been doing in the past hasn't worked should be more than enough motivation to make the change necessary to win. What you can't afford to do is look back on your life with regret but *still* make the same mistakes in the same way with the same outcome.

Your ex years represent a period in your life when you were blind to the seriousness of choosing wisely and you were unaware of the consequences. But now you have a way to see your past for what it is. A number that tells a story. Your story. A way to explore the truth about your past that cannot be fabricated or made up. Your number is your number, and now that you see it, what have you learned about yourself? What have you learned about others? What are you going to do about it?

Questions to ask yourself:

1. How many ex years do I have?
2. What does this number say about my success in relationships?
3. Based on this number, what should my next course of action be?
4. How would my life be different if I could relive those ex years?

10

The Pool

Imagine showing up at your local community center and deciding to go for a swim. You put on the proper attire, make sure you have on sunscreen, and you walk outside, ready to take a dip. You walk over to the pool only to discover that it is empty. No water, no nothing. Empty. You spot an employee on the other side of the pool sweeping up, and after walking over and commenting on the state of the pool, the employee casually walks over to the wall by the clubhouse and turns on one single garden hose. They throw one single garden hose into the pool, shoot you a thumbs up, smile, and say, "Enjoy!"

Question. Do you dive in?

Anyone with eyes can see that if you dive in now, there is no guarantee that you'll survive. Sure, there is a chance that if you dive in you won't be injured, but would you be able to dive in with any level of confidence? Would you be able to climb up onto the diving board knowing there is only a thin layer of water to cushion the fall?

For almost anyone, this would be an immediate, aggressive no. An empty pool in the middle of summer is a recipe for a bad day, and that's completely understandable. Who would jump into something and not know what the outcome would be? But as crazy as that sounds, it's exactly what we are doing when we don't take the time to be intentional about the people we let into our lives and get to know them on a deeper level before we commit to them. We are diving headfirst into an empty pool instead of being patient enough to wait for it to fill up.

The pool represents two things: the pool of knowledge you have about this person, which includes interactions, conversations, and general information you know, as well as how your personal experiences and life lessons align with this person's. The more we learn and grow with someone as friends, the more the pool fills up. And just like the pool on the hot summer day that was empty at first, eventually, you'll reach a point where you can confirm that it's safe to dive in based on tangible evidence, not emotion and feelings.

Yes, it is going to take a *very* long time to fill this thing up. You wanted what you wanted, and you wanted it *today*. But because you know what the outcome will be if you aren't careful, because you know diving into an empty pool just isn't a smart move, you'll contain your frustration and wait as long as it takes. Once you've verified from the safety of the ground that the pool is safe to dive into, you can get on top of the diving board, take a deep breath, and give it your best shot. If you jump any time before then, you can blame nobody but yourself for the aftermath.

Most people are diving into things headfirst and complaining after they hit the bottom of the empty pool. They have their minds set on swimming and not on mental, emotional, and physical well-being. People are getting married without even knowing things as simple as what their spouse's love languages are, or where they see themselves in five years, or how much debt they have. People are putting themselves in harm's way and continue to achieve the same results.

Additionally, the inconvenience of having to dry off from a dip in the pool adds insult to injury as the recovery process from an ill-advised swim is tedious, time-consuming, and takes an emotional toll on anyone. What hurts, even more, is when people who haven't even finished drying off from their last swim decide to hop into another pool that isn't safe to jump into yet.

Before you set your toe on the diving board, you need to do as much as you can to verify from the ground that the pool is filled with water. Knowing enough about this person to make a decision is crucial to diving in, and this is what gives you the confidence to step on the diving board and jump with a smile on your face. The more water in the pool, the better the swim. Let's get into how to understand when someone's pool is full.

II

Part Two

11

More Things To Consider

So here we are, having taken the time to review what we've done to arrive where we are. At this point, the hope is that you have gained clarity on the actions, thoughts, behaviors, and habits that you can change in order to make the best use of your time and intentions moving forward. However, before we discuss what Friends First looks and feels like, we must first take into consideration a few important principles that are meant to inject more knowledge into our lives and a little less feeling. Again, these ideas may sound unorthodox at first, but it will be good to ponder them moving forward. The goal is to begin thinking about things that perhaps you haven't in a way that can spark reflection and change.

Friends are the people who help shape the most important parts of who we become. From as early as you can remember, a good majority of your best memories probably involve friends. Regardless of whether you're still connected to those same people today or if those memories were made with people you only knew for a short while, the fact remains that friends are a key component in how we experience life.

Without friends, most of us would have very boring, uninteresting, and mundane stories to tell, or we'd have a stockpile of personal victories and accomplishments with no one to share them with. Without friends to help us vent and talk through our problems, we'd probably be very bad at expressing ourselves and communicating our feelings and emotions. We would also probably be very bad at operating in social circles, as we typically learn our social skills from within our sphere of influence before we get a chance to exercise those skills within the greater society.

If you think about it, friends are like an incubator where you get the chance to grow and cultivate yourself personally, and you use that incubation as a stepping stone for how you operate in other interpersonal environments for the rest of your life.

The bonds of friendship are not easily broken, but the bonds that hold together intimate relationships can sometimes be impossible to break. Therefore, we must approach this area of our lives with more care and more consideration than perhaps we understand. For most of us, we never learned how serious it is to make the right decisions in who our partner should be. The most we were taught was that if you like somebody and they like you, then you two must be together or should at least entertain the idea of being together.

But it's during this "entertaining each other" period that we get it wrong. Relationships have turned into a lottery. People playing their numbers, hoping it works, and suffering the consequences if it doesn't. We over-commit and get burned, or we under-commit and mixed signals get tossed around. You were given a formula for failure because the key component of friendship was never mentioned, and therefore you were put in a position where you were attempting to create a *lifelong* commitment with someone before you knew if they have even a lifelong friend. Hell, before you knew if they'd be a yearlong friend. Knowing how much our friends shape us and help us become who we are, but not requiring friendship as a non-negotiable before a serious, committed relationship is how we've gotten ourselves into this mess in the first place.

Let's dive into the deeper concepts of why becoming friends first is the best move you can make, and let's examine this approach from all angles.

12

The Friend Zone

Today, we have what's called the "friend zone." It's a place people are sent to when they don't qualify for relationship contention, and it's a place most people dread having to experience. The friend zone has become a long-standing, comical depiction of what happens when you meet someone but don't fall into their idea of what a good mate looks like to them. It's a place millennials fear and will try to avoid at all costs. Yes, there are funny videos about the friend zone. There are songs and podcasts and more memes than you can count. But have you ever thought about the benefits of the friend zone? Have you ever thought that perhaps we've been looking at it all wrong and that, with the proper definition, we can use the friend zone to our advantage?

Right now, there are some people who not only know who their soulmates or spouses are, but have met them, interacted with them, and have even hung out with them. But because they are so quick to jump from relationship to relationship without the proper fact-finding, and because they are so quick to prop someone in the "friend zone" without the proper context, they continue to postpone, sabotage, and derail the chance for them to connect with the one that would be perfect for them.

The friend zone shouldn't be a place where we simply send people who have no chance of dating us. Rather, the friend zone should be a place where you resign everyone you meet until further notice. We have romanticized and popularized the idea of a "sensational love experience," and if we don't feel a hot and heavy, exciting, thrilling, head-over-heels spark of love after a date or two, then we think that disqualifies that person from ever being with us. We have a very movie-like idea of what it means to meet the person you're meant to spend the rest of your life with.

Often, meeting the person you're meant to spend the rest of your life with is a slow, unexciting, drawn-out process that takes time, discernment, and patience. There's an old saying that says the same way you begin is the same way you end. And if you can be swept off your feet after a few dates and a rumble in the sheets, then you can just as easily be swept out of love and under the rug when someone decides you aren't exciting anymore. And you'll have to experience yet another breakup at the hands of hasty decision-making and the prioritizing of surface-level connection instead of cultivating deep, stable friendships.

When you are friends first with someone, you get the unique opportunity to see them in their natural state. They can act one way out in public, but behind closed doors, you get the chance to see that person without all of the bells and whistles and without the mask of political correctness that we all put on every single day. You see their good and bad habits; you learn about their relationships with family members and relatives; you learn how they feel about important things like marriage, religion, money, and success. And you get all of this in a relaxed, low-stakes environment.

You learn who they *really* are and what they *really* think. Likewise, when you marry someone, you are marrying the everyday version of that person. Becoming friends allows you to see this everyday version of them, the same version that you would be seeing if you were to spend the rest of your life with them. It's that simple.

So what does the "everyday" version of someone look like? It looks like getting into a relationship with someone who is put together on the outside, only to find that they live a junky, messy, and unorganized life at home. It's making a decision to commit to someone because they seem sexually compatible with you, only to have them give you less and less of what they used to and act as if you should be ok with it. The everyday version of someone is who and what they are after they get home from spending time with you. The person that bites their toenails, doesn't like spoons, or stays up until 1:00 a.m. every night. *That* is what you get when you choose to be with someone.

Friends shape you, too. There are certain habits, ideals, and beliefs that you can trace back to something a friend of yours said or did when you were much younger, and you still carry to this day. So in thinking about how friendships can have a lifelong impact on us, it would be in our best interest to put not just an emphasis, but an alarming priority on developing a true friendship with someone before taking a step in the direction of intimacy or exclusivity.

People tend to focus on the surface rather than substance and never take the time to ask questions that might disqualify someone from relationship eligibility simply because they check a few superficial boxes. Being friends with someone allows you to make a value judgment based on facts and not feelings. I know that when it comes to love and matters of the heart, we've subconsciously conditioned ourselves to believe that we should rely more on how we feel instead of relying on what we know to be fact.

I'm here to tell you that placing value on an emotional connection more so than placing value on tangible, real-world proof is dangerous. I'm here to tell you that you need to place a disproportionate amount of value on what you know about someone, and your feelings, good or bad, should be derived from those facts. Facts that need to be discovered within the confines of true friendship and not after you've fully committed. Facts that need to be discovered without the confusing banter that goes along with the current climate of dating and sex.

The friend zone isn't about discarding people who aren't attractive or don't have money or won't have sex with us. It's a place for everyone to be grouped until they can distinguish themselves as being worthy of more. The friend zone should be overflowing with names and numbers until you determine the one person who gets to experience life outside of that zone with you.

Keep in mind that this approach requires that you value yourself enough to withhold the benefits that go along with your company. You have to believe that what you have to offer and who you are is valuable enough to safeguard until the right person comes along. If you don't have that in place, then this updated friend zone approach will never work. Long story short, value yourself first, then keep your eyes peeled for someone who values you just as much.

Questions to ask yourself:

1. Are there people I've put in the friend zone who would actually be a good fit for me?
2. Do I have any healthy relationships with people that I would consider a potential mate?
3. How has the friend zone prevented me from connecting with people who would or could have been good for me to know?

13

The Anatomy of a Friend vs A Spouse

How can I be friends with someone without liking them? It's easy. Just think about your best friend. Take a moment and think about your closest one or two friends. The same way you developed those friendships should also be the exact way you develop a friendship with someone that could one day be "the one."

There are elements of having an intimate relationship that will not exist in a friendship, such as physical intimacy, public displays of affection, living together, and exclusivity, but I believe that the same qualities that make up a friend are the same qualities that make up a husband or wife. And it's those qualities from which the foundation for a lifelong connection grows.

One extra thing to note is that developing the ability to cultivate true, honest friendships with people is great practice for marriage. It allows you to develop positive habits that will translate well into the next stage in your relationship. The time to become well versed in healthy relationships is not after you get married and when the stakes are highest, but before.

So what makes up a friend? How does that overlap with being a good spouse?

Honesty

In friendships

The reason most people have close friends is that they can be honest with them. But this is a multilayered concept. When we think of our closest friends, we think of people who we can call on for honest advice and perspective, and we know they have our best interests at heart. But most importantly, this idea of honesty includes the fact that you and that other person can be honest about who you are when you are around each other.

You would not be friends with the people you associate with if you could not be honest about who you are and be your absolute self around them. It's what connects you. You don't have to like every single thing that they do, but if you have to pretend when you are around them, if you can't laugh about the same things, or if you can't be completely open about how you feel, then that friendship probably won't last.

My cousin, let's call him Keith, is my best friend and has been for several years. When he and I hang out together you would swear that we were biological brothers. We have an almost identical sense of humor, we enjoy the same video games, watching sports, cooking, beer, and traveling. We share a lot of the same views about women and relationships, and we can and have talked about everything under the sun.

We don't agree with each other about everything we discuss, but after we argue our respective points, we're able to move on without holding any grudges or allowing the differences that we do have to come between us. We can be completely honest with each other regardless of circumstance, and it's always been that way.

When you think about it, the reason that we become friends with the people that we do is that we can let our guard down and express the fullness of who we are while having the confidence that we'll be loved and accepted. This level of honesty is a necessity when it comes to harboring true friendship. Can you be honest in your dialogue, and can you be honest about who you are while with your friends? The answer should be yes, and it's what lays the foundation for a great friendship.

In marriage

A serious relationship, whether it be dating someone exclusively or marriage, will not and cannot survive for any length of time without honesty. Honesty in how you deal with problems, honesty in the things you say and do, and honesty in what it is that you want and need to have your needs met. If you can't be yourself around your partner, if you can't be authentic about how you feel and what your beliefs are, and if you can't be honest about what it is that you expect from this person and what you are willing to give to him or her, then you should throw in the towel today. It's that simple.

Honesty not only allows two people to operate confidently within a relationship, but it also insulates and protects any relationship from allowing small issues to fester and become big issues. Honesty breeds confidence in a relationship because it communicates that you are secure in yourself and are secure in standing by what makes you who you are. If you can't be honest and truthful with the one person you have chosen to spend the rest of your life with, who can you be honest with? If you are married or seriously involved, you will need to have honesty and lots of it.

Protection

In friendships

When we develop deep friendships with others, that often involves the cultivation of a sense of responsibility for their well-being. The "you're not fighting, *we're* fighting" mentality begins to grow, and any problems that they have become your problems. You're willing to fight for them, speak up on their behalf, and otherwise uphold their name, whether they are with you in person or not.

It's human nature to protect what we value, and when the friendship ties begin to run deep, that sense of protection begins to grow until it reaches the point where there's nothing you wouldn't do to make sure that your friends know you would sacrifice your well-being for theirs — your physical well-being, financial well-being, so on and so forth.

In marriage

We protect the things we value most. Our homes, our vehicles, our businesses, our finances, and ultimately, our relationships. When you say you're in a serious relationship with someone, what you're also silently communicating is that you are serious about protecting this person physically, financially, emotionally, and mentally. While there is a level of protection involved in friendship, that protection is broader and less refined, if you will. However, the protection afforded in marriage is acute, specific, and exclusive to one person — forever. For example, you might help your friend if they needed to borrow a couple of dollars, but would you list them as the beneficiary on your life insurance? Would you add them to your health insurance? See the difference?

A spouse is the one person who you have taken an oath to protect above all others. A spouse is someone who compels you to change the way you approach certain situations, someone who makes you become more vigilant, and more importantly, someone who makes you guard your heart against people and situations that could come between you two.

When it comes to your spouse, there should be a sense of pride in knowing that you are taking care of their needs, providing for them (whether it be financially or emotionally), and that you are providing a safe space for them to be who they are at all times. When you're married to someone, there should and will be a protective instinct that kicks in when it comes to making sure your partner is safe. No protection, no marriage.

Growth

In friendships

People who spend time together naturally grow together. This is especially true for those we hold near and dear to us. As friends, you and those close to you will naturally grow in your maturity, your ambition, your connection to one another, and your mutual acquaintances. You will help each other deal with loss and heartbreak, and they will watch as you reach a new level of achievement in your personal and professional life. Growth will and should happen with those you call friends. If you are friends at twenty-one, you should not be doing the same things and living the same life as you did when you reach thirty-five.

What helps you draw closer to your friends is the sense of progress and the culture of camaraderie that develops over a long period. You celebrate each other's victories and continue to formulate plans on how to bounce back from losses and use them as learning experiences. You grow deeper in your ability to be honest even when it hurts, and you can be transparent and vulnerable about things that you struggle with.

Growth in friendship is necessary and is the fabric of what holds you two together. Your interests, similarities, and chemistry are what connect you, but growth is what bonds you. It's what molds you into something greater and more substantial. Without growth, friendship won't stand the time.

In marriage

In a marriage, growth is not only inevitable but also completely necessary for a continued sense of connection and bonding. Think about how much you've changed and grown as a person since you were born — from early childhood development to puberty to achieving financial stability and experiencing new levels of emotional maturation. We have all grown in some respects.

When it comes to a spouse, you will grow both as individuals and as a unit. You and your spouse will experience personal growth and change as you experience life, learn from your mistakes, and reflect on life lessons, and in that, you two will grow as a couple as you navigate the ever-changing dynamic of living with someone, sharing your possessions, dealing with life's ups and downs, and planning for your future.

Each moment of growth fuels the growth of your relationship and vice versa as you pull from one to guide and shape the other. A marriage must have growth for it to stay fresh, exciting, and relevant for what life brings. Lots of divorces occur simply because two people believe they fell out of love. If we were to take a deeper look, we'd probably discover that they simply hadn't experienced any growth together as a couple *or* that they didn't believe that their spouse was someone they could grow with. Either way, when you choose to spend a lifetime with someone, growth is a necessity, not an option. As life and circumstances change, so should you and your spouse.

Vulnerability

In friendships

To have a friend or be a friend, you have to be vulnerable. You have to trust that when you are dealing with issues that make you feel defeated or inadequate, you can turn to that person and know with absolute certainty they won't abuse the power of knowing the intimate details of your life.

Vulnerability can be the scariest place for some people because when you are vulnerable with people, you are giving them power. The power to either help you or hurt you. To speak life into you or to speak death. You are giving them the ability to build you up during a moment of weakness or an opportunity to affirm those self-limiting beliefs that we all have as humans.

Can you be vulnerable to your friends? Do you trust that they'll handle sensitive information with care and tact? Or do you insulate yourself from the possibility that they might abuse this power by never discussing real issues? Do you engage in surface talk, or are you comfortable with discussing real things that you deal with? If you can be vulnerable with someone, odds are you and that person are friends.

In marriage

Marriage is meant to last a lifetime. Two people. One marriage. One lifetime. That being said, during this lifetime together, two people must create an environment that encourages and rewards vulnerability. The person you choose to spend the rest of your life with must be someone you can tell everything to. Your flaws, your insecurities, your inadequacies, your fears, and anything else that puts you in a position to be judged or chastised.

You have to have someone next to you who not only accepts you when you're vulnerable but doesn't abuse or take advantage of those private moments when you let your guard down and open up to them. When two people can experience vulnerability with each other, it strengthens the bonds of their marriage and creates a partnership based on trust and honesty. A spouse is someone who should make you feel safe no matter what it is you have to tell them because you know that they will handle you with care and concern, not judgment and disappointment.

Marriage is not something temporary, and within that, the need for vulnerability and an environment that doesn't punish you for it is what cultivates confidence for the life of the covenant that two people create. Vulnerability is a vital part of the dynamic between spouses and is one of the healthiest ways to continue to grow together as a couple.

No competition

In friendships

Friendship is not a competition, nor should it ever be. It's good to become motivated by the accomplishments of those closest to you and to use their achievements to help fuel your desire to do more in your own life, but friendship is not a contest. If you are only keeping someone around to serve as a measuring stick of what you should and should not do, something is off. More importantly, if the only reason you keep someone around as a "friend" is to show off and boost your ego because you have more accomplishments and material possessions than they do, then something is *really* off.

As a friend, you should be able to celebrate the positives and accolades of others without feeling diminished in your own life. Without feeling less than. You shouldn't hug them when they win and frown when you get in your car to drive home. You shouldn't celebrate their promotion and then chronicle all the reasons why you should have what they have the entire Uber ride home.

Friends don't compete. Friends collaborate. Friends run their race in life while at the same time asking how they can help each other accomplish everything they're aiming for in life. A friend says, "Congratulations on the awards. How can we get you to the next one?"

In marriage

Your spouse is not someone you should compete with. There should be no instances of you feeling like you need to one-up your partner. Another way of saying this is that there should be no jealousy, feelings of wanting to get even, or wanting to steal the spotlight. Yes, your spouse might experience a level of success greater than yours. Yes, your spouse may accomplish their goals faster than you do or they may accomplish more goals than you do. Yes, your spouse may do things that you can't. But at the end of the day, unless you're trying to outdo them in the area of giving or supporting, then there should never be a time where you're in competition for anything.

Remember, marriage is a team effort, and your accomplishments are for the benefit of the team, not just you.

No agenda

In friendships

The best part about friendship is the absence of agendas. Too often we see people become "friends" to gain social status, increase their pool of potential clients, garner future referrals, and otherwise serve their interests. We see people develop temporary, surface-level relationships, and the moment they realize that they won't get what they need, they disappear. This isn't to say that every single person you meet is meant to stay in your life forever, but the beauty of developing long-lasting, fruitful friendships is that there are no agendas.

Agenda-free friendship is a beautiful thing. Two people who simply want to be in each other's lives for no other reason but to add as much value as possible and take as little as possible. Two people who will quickly look for ways to help one another without ever asking, expecting, or needing anything in return. Two people who give without hesitation. Two people who admit when they are wrong and quickly find a way to resolve any differences they may have so that they can move forward together. When you don't have an agenda, you open yourself up to a world of possibilities because you are viewing others through the lens of genuine connection and not opportunity.

When you don't have an agenda, you are ok with taking the backseat when it's their time to shine because you know that when it's your turn, they'll be right there yelling your name the loudest. When you don't have an agenda, you aren't plagued by jealous or envious thoughts, and you celebrate their wins as if they are your own.

In marriage

As a married man or woman, there should be no hidden agendas. Unfortunately, some people do get married for selfish reasons, and as soon as they get what they came for, whether it be money, fame, or social connections, they change for the worse or file for divorce. It's sad, but, as you should know, it's not what marriage is all about. As a spouse, there should be no hidden agendas. You should be confident in your choice of man or woman, you should be open and honest about what it is you want and need from the relationship, and you should feel comfortable being vulnerable and transparent about the ups and downs of life.

You should not get married because your potential spouse knows famous people. You should not get married because you are desperate and just need someone to cling to. And you should not get married as a way to prove to your family that you have finally found love after all these years of screwing relationships up. Marrying someone should not be a way to make others jealous and should not be a competition between you and your friends. Marriage should not be a tool to achieve some hidden purpose that your spouse doesn't know about. A spouse will be authentically and genuinely with you and for you in every capacity.

Help

In friendships

Your friends should help you. Period. Yes, they should listen to your ideas and give you positive feedback. Yes, they should be a listening ear in times of hardship or doubt, and they should offer constructive criticism when needed. Yes, a friend should cheer you on from the sidelines when it's your time to shine and tell everyone they know how amazing you are when you reach new goals and milestones in your life.

But...that's not enough. Your friends should help you in concrete, tangible ways and demonstrate through action their friendship with you. If you open up a catering business, you should have friends who not only say, "Hey, that's great that you opened up your first business," but who follow it up with, "I can help serve customers if you need me on Saturdays."

Friends root for you on the sidelines, but also get in the game and run a few plays with you to let you know that they are in this with you. If you have a friend who *never* shows up to your functions or never takes any action to support you, then you might need to take a second look at that person. Yes, life can get hectic, and people are busier now more than ever, but friends aren't friends from a distance. Friends roll up their sleeves (literally) and jump in with you. Your friends should help you.

In marriage

As a spouse, it's not only your job to support your partner with words and affirmations, but when it's time to get down and dirty, a big part of marriage is help! Not just supporting your mate from the sidelines as they try to accomplish their goals and dreams, but real, actual, tangible, physical help that they can see. As a spouse, it's not enough to play a passive role in the life of your partner. It's your job to actively assist and help when and how your partner needs it. Cook a few meals, stay up late so they can grab a few extra hours of sleep, listen to their ideas and offer some of your own, pick up the kids even if it's inconvenient, and so much more. A spouse offers help when it's needed the most and doesn't keep score.

We can be very picky with our friends. Perhaps too picky at times. Most of us will only allow a certain number of people at a time to reach friend status, and an even smaller number of people will *ever* receive the coveted title of "best friend." We only allow a tiny handful of individuals to have access to the best parts of us — our time, resources, attention, money, and consideration. Both because it would be impossible to allocate ourselves to whoever floats in and out of our lives, and also because we realize early on that not everyone has our best interests at heart.

When it comes to friends, we take our time to develop these relationships and are quick to cut people off when we realize that they are disingenuous, needy, selfish, proud, negative, or toxic. We never set a time limit on how long it should take to develop this dynamic with others, and we never set exceptions on what the friendship should be. We're not going to be indifferent about what our friends say or do, but we don't come in the gate imposing any hidden agendas. Simply put, we're never "looking for a friend." We let friendships happen, and during this process, we preserve those connections that serve us and eventually discard what we know cannot be used.

When it comes to finding the one person you'll go the distance with, you can make a direct correlation between what you should look for in a friend and what you should look for in a mate. We tend to want to separate the two and treat them as mutually exclusive situations. We believe that if someone is too much of a friend, they reach a threshold that eliminates them from relationship eligibility, which is one of the biggest reasons why we get things so wrong.

The qualities that we are ultimately looking for in a future spouse are the exact qualities we experience with our closest friends, but we never make the connection. It doesn't have to be one or the other, friend or lover, homie or girlfriend or boyfriend. This is an instance where you can most definitely have your cake and eat it too. At the end of the day, a marriage is a lifelong commitment, and to make that lifelong commitment a successful one, we need to understand the anatomy of a spouse and commit to finding someone who fits that mold and fits it well. Marriage is not just more of what you've experienced during the dating phase. It's a chance to create a legacy with someone and build something that lasts forever.

Questions to ask yourself:

1. Do my current friendships mirror what a healthy friendship should look like?
2. Do my serious relationships tend to mirror what a healthy friendship looks like?
3. Which areas of friendship do I tend to omit or overlook?
4. For all of the relationships that haven't gone the distance, are there any specific areas that could be the cause?

14

Can We Just Be Friends?

Now that we've gone over just how much a solid friendship overlaps with having a solid marriage, you might be asking, "Can men and women be friends?" I mean, seriously. Can a man and a woman spend a lengthy amount of time together and become legitimate friends without falling victim to the pitfalls of sexual attraction and simple biology?

The answer is yes and no. It's yes because we all have friends of the opposite sex that we have never been intimate with or have never had the urge to be intimate with. We all have friends that we've known for quite some time who have remained just that. But, with all things, there is another side to the coin. It's a no because we naturally tend to associate with people who share our same interests and viewpoints and who will naturally cause some level of chemistry or connection, even if it's mild.

Also, most of us will very quickly take the same scenario and have two different trains of thought depending on who we're talking to. For example, if you are a guy and you meet another guy through a mutual friend, and you discover that this guy knows just as much about football as you do, then your thought process might be something as simple as, "Hey, this guy knows a lot about football. We should probably grab a beer sometime on college game day."

On the other hand, if you are a guy and you meet a girl who knows just as much about football as you do, your thought process may be, "Man, it's kind of sexy that she knows so much about football. We should grab a beer sometime on college game day and maybe I'll get a chance to hit that."

It won't happen like this in every case. But when we're talking about attraction, we tend to subconsciously see favorable, unique, or positive character traits as a reason to like someone instead of just a reason to get to know them as a friend. As soon as we discover that she likes video games, all of a sudden, we think she's wifey, or as soon as we find out that he makes $100,000 per year, we're thinking he could be the one. At this point, the question is how do you *not* see positive character traits as a reason to like that person, and how do you just remain friends?

At the end of the day, the determining factor as to whether or not a guy and a girl can be friends without anything else happening is simply the motive that exists at the onset of the friendship. If you find it difficult to interact with someone without wanting something from them, then that may be the issue. Whether it's sex, time, or affection, you can't walk into a new friendship trying to see what you can get.

Trying to see how they can benefit you and facilitate the needs you have at the moment is not how friendships form, and that's not how friendships are maintained. To stay friends with someone and truly remain that way, there has to be a conscious choice on your part to not see that person as a resource you can tap into when you need a void filled. You need to see them as someone you're in the process of getting to know, simply to get to know them. No more, no less.

Friends, Not Just "Friend-ly"

When it comes to developing a relationship with someone, we have to make the distinction between being an actual friend and simply being friendly. A lot of us don't know what it means to be a friend with someone of the opposite sex without wanting something from them or secretly admiring them. We'll typically separate people into two different categories: people who we would never date for any reason, and people we are attracted to and would like to see if they are attracted to us.

What ends up happening is that we don't become friends. We just become friendly. We display general, likable characteristics that can be considered nice to the average person. We call and text them more often, and we give off friendly vibes without a real friendship as the desired outcome.

Understand that as soon as you have convinced yourself that you like someone even the smallest iota, your behavior towards them will be different than the behavior you exhibit towards others. Being friendly but not being friends is how a lot of us get hurt and how a lot of us hurt others. The reason being is because friendliness and friendship have very similar and overlapping qualities that can sometimes make it hard to determine if someone in your life is genuinely interested in you as a person or if they want something from you. That something they want can be anything from sex and companionship to money or control.

Either way, being friendly is not the same thing as being an actual friend. Likewise, if you enter into a relationship with the sole objective of actually becoming someone's friend, then it's much easier to refrain from transitioning into a full-fledged relationship because that was never your intent to begin with. Wanting to become someone's friend without the thought of "what if" is the first step towards avoiding mixed signals and emotional connections that aren't mutual or warranted.

During this period of cultivating friendships, it's important to note that you need to shift your focus from trying to qualify friendships into potential relationships and simply focus on the friendship itself.

Here's how to do this:

1. FOCUS - Focus on being an actual friend. Ask questions about their life. What they do. How they think. What they know. Become interested in them, not what they can or could do for you at some point in the future.
2. THINK - Get out of your own head. Let go of the idea that just because someone is attractive, you must investigate further. Honestly, there will *always* be another attractive person. Does that mean you need to shoot your shot with all of them? Of course not! So maturing in this area is key. Until you know who they are, their appearance is of no consequence. Focus on who they are and not what they look like.
3. REFLECT - Understand your triggers and have the self-awareness to think logically about what has caused you to stumble in the past and what about this person could cause you to make the same mistake again.

Look for Friends, Not Potential Mates

It's subtle, but attempting to look at friendship as something that has the potential to become more will still cause you to subconsciously operate in a way that can sabotage whatever could have been there. For example, after meeting someone at a bookstore and grabbing coffee, the week after you're already telling your friends that this person has potential, and as soon as you do that, you have already made the shift from a friendship into just being friendly.

It's innocent, but the difference is that friendship exists simply for the sake of the friendship, whereas being friendly occurs when you already have an end game in mind. The goal here is not to think about what could be or how many great qualities this person has or even how compatible you two could be for each other. The goal here is to simply become somebody's friend until further notice, just like you do with the other friends you currently have in your life. So to answer the question a different way, *yes!* A man and a woman can be strictly friends with each other if the two have friendship as the core motive for getting to know each other. Anything more and we've already lost before we've begun.

Questions to ask yourself:

1. Do I subscribe to the notion that people can actually be friends without wanting something from each other? Why or why not?
2. Where have I struggled in the past when it comes to remaining friends with someone rather than pursuing something more serious?

3. Do I have a habit of being friend-ly in an attempt to get what I want from someone?
4. Have I ever been friends with someone with no strings attached? What was the outcome?

Action plan:

Create an action plan to refer to in the future by taking a moment to answer the following sections that are designed to empower you to not only be aware of what to do when it comes to making true friendships, but how and why when the time is right. Grab a sheet of paper and pen if you need them.

What are three things I will do to cultivate friendships in a healthy, productive way?

For the people who I am interested in, would it make sense to pull back and learn more about them instead?

For anyone who I'm interested in, what five questions should I be asking them that would help me to pursue them with confidence and intent, rather than a "let's see what happens" vibe?

15

Friends First: Pros vs Cons

Taking the road less traveled and becoming friends first has its pros and cons, and these are things you must be aware of. Like anything in life, there will be things about being friends first that are amazing, and there will be things about being friends first that are frustrating and may cause you to doubt the whole process. If you think focusing on being friends first is a strategy you should adopt, then here are the pros and cons you need to be aware of.

Pros

Fewer dates
Less heartbreak and disappointment
More friends
Confidence when it's time
Time to be alone

~ ~ ~

Cons

Fewer dates
FOMO
Time to be alone
Goes against pop culture

Pros

Fewer Dates

If you choose to subscribe to the *Friends First* approach to finding your next serious relationship, one thing you can look forward to is going on much fewer dates. For a man, this means spending less money, not needing to impress anyone, and not having to "hunt" for anything at the end of the night. In all honesty, when a man goes on a date, he's looking for one of two things: a wife or a hookup. He'll take whatever is presented to him, but the truth is that usually a date results in a hookup or an attempt to hook up that is met with a stiff no. This hookup or hunt mentality is precisely what makes dating so destructive to how men interact with women, and less of this is a great thing.

For a woman, this means less having to get ready for two hours, only to be disappointed by the guy you thought had the potential to be "the one." It means no more taking an optimistic position about something you can't confidently say is going to turn out well. No more rolling the dice again. When we say yes to being friends first, what we are saying yes to is the idea that a date is no more an indication of whether you and someone else should be together than is a tarot card reading from Miss Cleo herself. They both have their novelty but are not a strong indicator of anything.

One of the great things about choosing to be friends first is that you no longer have to fall victim to the unproductive and unreliable side effects of dating, and you can instead focus on meeting people without having to pretend to be someone you aren't or pretend you like someone when you don't. What's worse than going on a date knowing you have something to hide, but not knowing whether or not they have something to hide, and acting as if all is well? That's a tightrope we walk all too often that has led a lot of us down the path of failure time and time again.

What's the use of going out on a date with someone when you don't know who he or she is? Likewise, what can one evening teach you about somebody that being friends first can't? The crazy thing is that adhering to current dating norms will have you discarding people from the pool of eligible partners for all the wrong reasons and at the same time have you choosing people for the wrong reasons. One date typically won't tell you what you need to know, yet we will make a judgment call as if it does.

Less Heartbreak and Disappointment

I think that we could all stand to experience less heartbreak and disappointment, yet we continue to put ourselves in a position to receive just that. We continue to date people we don't know, and we continue to be dishonest with ourselves and others about what we want or what we don't want. Up until now, most of us have either been disappointed time and time again either because of dates that went nowhere or relationships that crashed and burned. And most of us have experienced at least one major heartbreak, the kind of heartbreak that left you emotionally devastated, financially wiped out, confused, angry, and wondering why things happened the way they did. When you choose to become friends first, all of that changes.

Becoming friends first allows you to experience less disappointment because, from the beginning, your expectations of this person make it impossible for them to disappoint you. The reason we experience so much hurt and frustration is because we come in the door with high hopes and play a role in our failures when it comes to finding the one. When we like someone and then use that alone as the basis for wanting to go on a date or date someone exclusively, we are sharpening the knife that's going to stab us in the side later.

We are placing expectations on people we don't know and on a situation that we can't say for certain will be fruitful. We are setting ourselves up for the fall and then blaming the other person for not being who we thought they would be. Eventually, we are involved in a cycle of liking, dating, and disappointment. We like someone for surface reasons, we date them to find out more, and we end up disappointed, frustrated, and angry when we discover they aren't it. And then we wonder why we're having so much trouble finding a good guy or a great girl.

Becoming friends first is all about prioritizing knowing who someone is before liking them, loving them, or placing any labels on them that cause us to give them the benefit of the doubt before they deserve it. Friends first says, "Let me learn as much as I can so that when the time is right, we can move forward with confidence instead of hope and intangibles."

And let's make one thing clear: becoming friends first is not operating from a position of weakness or fear, but rather from a position of strength, wisdom, and confidence. It's only logical that you would have less disappointment if you knew the person sitting across from you. Like I said earlier in this book, you don't date to get to know someone, you get to know someone so that you can date. That's a great formula for experiencing less disappointment and enjoying the dating process moving forward.

More Friends

There's a reason the word "friends" is plural in the title of this book. To find the one, you need to make more than one friend. You'd be wise to make as many friends as you possibly can in the pursuit of finding the one you're meant to be with. And one beautiful but overlooked side effect of getting to know people is that you'll make more friends! Understand that if you spend ten years getting to know people from all of your different social circles and groups, and you make connections in your respective career field and industry, not only will you increase your chance of finding your future partner, but you'll make lots of friends along the way instead of making lots of exes.

Rather than date five guys in ten years, experience five breakups, and marry the sixth, you can make twenty friends in ten years and marry the twenty-first. What this means is less heartbreak, more connections, and more insight into what you're looking for in someone without having to push your chips to the middle of the table and go all in.

Think about your last relationship. What did you learn? You probably learned more about what you don't want in a man or woman, but what positive things did you take away from a situation that didn't work out? If you ask a group of people that question, you might hear answers like, "Mark taught me about the value of reading every day," or "John encouraged me to get my passport and travel more."

These are all positives, and while it's great that you learned something, realize that most of what you learned from your failed relationships are things that you could have easily learned without being in a relationship with that person. It's true. You can still learn things about life and love, and you can still absorb nuggets of wisdom and insight from people without inviting them into your bedroom and/or life. I submit to you that you could still be the person you are right now without having to go through what you've been through. Choosing to be friends first is what can allow you to do that. While developing friendships, you are able to ask all of the deep questions you want and are able to expand your relationship palette without the consequences of committing to someone.

For example — you meet someone and ask them, "How do you react when you don't get your way?" You listen to their response, have a great dialogue about the subject, discuss how you react as well, and then take mental notes about whether or not that is something you would or wouldn't tolerate in a relationship. This conversation adds to the amount of information you know about the person sitting across from you and allows you to continue your friendship (or not) without any hiccups in your life or theirs. Sounds easy enough, right?

What we typically do is discover how our partner handles conflict while smack-dab in the middle of the relationship and on autopilot, and if the answer is something that eventually becomes a dealbreaker for us, we then have to go through the painful process of another breakup, more injuries from the inevitable fall, and another few notches added to our ex years belt. In both scenarios, we learned something about the other person, but one scenario results in a deeper understanding of ourselves and others, and the other scenario results in disaster. Which one sounds more appealing?

Friends first emphasizes natural, unforced connection and information instead of love and intuition. And the more people you meet and the more you focus on cultivating meaningful relationships, the more you'll learn in the process, minus the negatives of being with someone that you were never meant to be with.

Hypothetically speaking, if you date three men in ten years, that is only three opportunities to learn from others and grow in relationships. Let's be honest — once most of us get into a relationship, we tend to drop all other potentials. However, in that same ten-year period, if you were single and looking for the right one, you could benefit from the knowledge and friendship of as many people as time and opportunity would allow you to meet without limiting yourself to just one person at a time.

Confidence When It's Time

You know that feeling you get when you've prepared for something and the day you've been waiting for finally arrives? That feeling knowing that you studied or did all the necessary preparations and now you get a chance to see all your hard work come together? When the time comes, you feel confident, in control, and ready. Not nervous, but anxious to see all your hard work come to fruition. Excited about how everything will turn out when it's all said and done. We've all been there. But can you say you've been there in your relationships?

Have you ever been on the cusp of a new relationship and felt confident in your choice? Not a pseudo-prepared, "I hope this works out" feeling, but an "I know this will work and I can't wait to get started" feeling. Being friends first and laying the foundation for your relationships through fact-finding, extended interaction, objective thinking, and honesty is what gives you the confidence to enter into a relationship knowing what the result will be.

How many times have you asked your friends or family members how things are going in their relationships only to hear a vague, indifferent, depressing, lackluster response? Things like "We're just hanging in there" or "It is what it is"? You may brush it off, but I urge you to pay attention to the confidence, or lack thereof, in their voice. It's a clear testament to how they feel about the relationship as a whole.

What typically happens is we tend to front-load every relationship with feelings of euphoria and high hopes only to reach a plateau when we inevitably realize we don't have the confidence to move forward. Being friends first operates like compound interest in the way that it starts at zero and slowly escalates until much further down the line the amount of confidence you have grows exponentially when it's time to decide to be together. It requires patience and self-control, both of which people struggle with. But the payoff outweighs the process tenfold.

Time to Yourself

For one reason or another, more and more people are finding it hard to be by themselves. When it comes to flying solo, people often use the term "alone" by default. But the word "alone" has a negative, depressing context and implies that there is an inherent, unavoidable lack in not having someone else with you at all times.

We've become so connected that when we aren't interacting

with something or someone, we feel like something is missing. Contrary to the current state of pop culture, spending time with yourself is one of the best things you can do for your health, your sanity, and your relationships. In the *Friends First* world, during the time you are getting to know others and develop friendships, what you'll also be able to take advantage of is time to yourself. Time you can use to hone in on what you want from a partner and life as a whole.

Time is our greatest enemy and our greatest ally. Rather, time spent poorly is our greatest enemy, and time spent wisely is our greatest ally. When you are single, it is not a time to wallow in your own self-pity. It is not a time to wake up every morning wondering what's wrong with you and why you can't find "the one." When you are single, it is time to take action! It is your chance to figure out what changes you need to make in your life that will push you forward towards whatever goals or aspirations you have. It's time to focus.

As a single person, this time can be used to save money, move to a new city, rekindle old passions, drop that forty pounds, dedicate more time and energy to your goals and dreams, and become the architect of your life. Time spent in relationships that serve no long-term purpose is time wasted, and with connectivity on the rise, the best way to find what you're looking for is to do your own thing for a while.

Don't look at being single as a period of loneliness, but attribute this period of getting to know people as a season of rebuilding, adjusting, learning, and planning. Part of why relationships fail is due to a lack of being prepared, and taking time to yourself is what will position you for success when the time comes for you to allow someone to enjoy the benefits of being with you and vice versa. Perhaps you're familiar with the notion of being "whole" — the belief that you should know what you want to do with your life, that you should have an intimate relationship with yourself, and should be actively dealing with a lot of the issues we've picked up in life before you can truly offer yourself to someone else. Otherwise, you can potentially sabotage that relationship, as this sabotage will manifest itself through arguments, secrecy, toxic habits, and more.

The best way to deal with these issues and become whole is by spending time with oneself, focusing on those things that serve as barriers to our happiness, and making an effort to change. You have to realize that success in relationships is equally a factor of changes made during a relationship as well as changes made before the relationship even begins. Being friends first allows you to continue to learn about others while giving you the freedom to continue to learn about yourself.

Cons

Fewer Dates

One of the cons of becoming friends first with others is that you'll go on fewer dates. Much fewer dates. Like, no dates at all. You'll have to give up the glitz and the glam of "the date" and replace it with interactions that facilitate getting to know someone on a genuine, authentic level. What this means is that you'll have to give up the superficial for something a bit more meaningful.

No, dates aren't the only way to meet someone or get to know them. No, going on a date is not a strong indicator of whether or not someone is compatible with you. No, dates shouldn't be something that automatically take place just because you have a couple of things in common.

Yes, blind dates are the worst idea ever. No, going on fewer dates doesn't necessarily mean it will take longer to find the right one. It just means you'll make fewer bad decisions along the way.

Granted, dates can be fun. It is exciting to meet someone new and enjoy a meal and put on your Sunday best. It's refreshing to meet someone who shares similar interests and whose goals and ambitions align with yours. Absolutely yes. The idea of this person potentially being "the one" is electrifying, if I may use that word, and after a date that goes extremely well, we're left feeling optimistic that we could finally have hit the jackpot.

But take a moment and think about the last time a great first or second date turned into a third date, which turned into more time together, which turned into sex, which turned into dating exclusively, which turned into living together, which turned into problems and the eventual realization that you were incompatible, which eventually turned into a breakup that left you drained and frustrated.

It's at that point you have to realize that great first dates can still lead to heartbreak and are no guaranteed indication of relationship success. So no, you won't go on many dates while you focus on being friends first, but looking at how things have transpired in the past, it's best to look at the long-term goal of compatibility and relationship success versus the short-term enjoyment of a date that has a solid chance of going nowhere.

FOMO

Fear of missing out is a real thing. More commonly known as FOMO, many of us operate with an underlying spirit of not wanting to miss the next best thing. Whether it be a new hit series or annual awards show, a new car or house, the latest viral sensation, or the next dance move, we want to be in the know about current trends and events.

More seriously, however, when we miss the wave, we can very easily begin to feel inadequate. If you were to scroll down your Instagram timeline right this moment, you would see everyone you know living their best life, making a home video trying to participate in the newest "challenge," enjoying a two-week vacation in Fiji, getting married, or buying their first home.

You'll see nothing but people's high moments. Moments of happiness, success, and achievement. At first, you'll smile and maybe even like their photo, but after you put the phone down and reality sets in, you realize that you're still stuck at the job you don't like, and your bank account still has $91.54 in it.

That's when FOMO hits. You start to feel like everyone on the other side of your phone screen is winning and winning big, and you're missing out on life. You start to feel a serious sense of lack in your life and it makes you feel like if you aren't doing exactly what they're doing, that you are somehow less. This is the same feeling you'll have to deal with when you decide to be friends first. Everyone around you will be going on dates and enjoying vacations and moving in together. Everyone will have a #mancrushmonday or a #womancrushwednesday, and it will bother you.

Even if you know that some of the people you see aren't right for each other, it will still bother you because while you're sitting at home, they're out in the public eye enjoying the benefits of having a relationship, such as intimacy, quality time, and PDA. This is when you need to fight the urge to jump into a relationship in haste. It's at this moment you'll start to say things like, "I've been single too long, it's time to find someone," or "It sure would be nice to have what they have."

FOMO will cause you to make the biggest mistakes of your life if you are not keenly aware of your triggers, become caught up in the moment, and make the decision to jump into the pool when it is not safe to do so. Keep in mind that although you will continue to see others living their "best lives," your focus needs to be on the ultimate prize and not just a participation trophy.

Time to Be Alone

When you choose to be friends first, what you're also choosing is to be single for an extended period until you know enough about someone to confidently begin a relationship. Naturally, this means that you will spend a lot of time by yourself as you start to meet new people, cultivate relationships, and get to know others. This is where people will begin to feel as though something is wrong. Not because there is something wrong, but because being single for an extended period makes people feel like something is off.

Being by ourselves isn't something we would prioritize over having someone with us if we have the choice to, and being single for an extended period subconsciously makes us prone to feeling something we can't quite describe but are certain is real. Being by yourself has its rough patches. There will be nights where you just wish you had someone to hold or talk to. There will be days where you wish you could call someone up and be able to tell them you love them. You'll have moments of weakness where you are tempted to pick up the phone and call someone that you know you shouldn't or do things you know aren't in your best interest.

Being by yourself will magnify our insecurities, as it forces you to deal with a lot of the things that you struggle with by yourself. When you're single, you don't have financial help from a significant other, you have no one to help take care of you when you're sick, no one is there to speak your love languages and help you through a stressful day, and no one there to tell you it's going to be ok. You're out there making things work by yourself, and you don't have anyone to fall back on for support, encouragement, guidance, or reassurance.

Yes, being single long term isn't all roses, and some days will be much harder than others. As with everything in life, you simply have to decide if this solo time is worth it. During this time of being single, you must make the critical distinction of being single versus being lonely. These are two very different things. More specifically, you need to ask yourself, "Is this solo time worth making the right choice in who I want to spend the rest of my life with?" The answer, I hope, is yes.

Goes Against Pop Culture

Being friends first goes against pop culture. There's a certain fun that pop culture has attributed to the dating scene in that it glamorizes it and makes us numb to how serious choosing the right person is. If Hollywood was the blueprint for what relationships should look like, we'd all have a new boyfriend or girlfriend every six months, at least one divorce, and a tattoo of at least one ex somewhere on our arm. It's what we see almost every single day in the news, on YouTube, in tabloids, in music videos, and in comedy.

You meet someone, hook up within a week, make your relationship as public as possible, endure a "fiery" breakup, and then meet someone again in a few short months.

If you aren't careful, pop culture will lead you to believe that the most toxic things you can do in your relationship are things that help the most. How many times have you seen someone go through a divorce or breakup, and as soon as they meet someone else their entire social media is overflowing with pictures, provocative videos, selfies, and #baecation hashtags?

Although this behavior is partly due to our innate desire to make people jealous or to hurt people who hurt us, a big part of this is because of what we see from people in the public eye. Making every private part of your relationship public for the world to see without any shame, tact, or censorship whatsoever.

When was the last time you heard anyone brag about how they were friends first and got to know someone before they even went on a date? When was the last time you heard someone repeatedly and insistently encourage others to slow down and get to know as much as possible about someone? Just about every blue moon, you may see a video from a B-list celebrity advocating for actually knowing someone before committing to them, but for the most part, it's something that never gets mentioned or discussed in grave detail.

Being friends first goes against the grain of our current dating culture, and for good reason. It's not glamorous, it doesn't provide instant gratification, and it's something that shouldn't happen quickly. All that being said, why would you want it any other way? When you are laying the foundation for what should be a lifelong commitment, a few dates, sex, and a tattoo on your left wrist shouldn't be enough to say yes. If you aren't careful, pop culture will have you feeling like you're doing something wrong by not being reckless in how you go about choosing your next partner.

At the end of it all, choosing to be friends first is just that: a choice. Knowing what goes along with this choice is incredibly important and will certainly make all of the difference. Knowing that when you choose to gather information on the front end as opposed to the back end of a serious commitment, you are choosing to do what others will think is unnecessary, silly, or ineffective. You need to make up in your mind that you will be single until you connect with someone in a real way *before* you give yourself to them in any serious manner, and you need to understand that it will not be a perfect walk in the park. But it will be worth it in every way.

Questions to ask yourself:

1. Am I clear on the pros and cons that go along with becoming friends first with others?
2. Which pros of becoming friends first am I looking forward to the most?
3. Which cons of friends first will I struggle with the most?

16

The 'No' List

Let's set some ground rules for what it takes to truly be friends first with someone *before* you two are exclusive. In life, there are times when we need to simply say no. Believe it or not, saying no can save your life if you know when, and more importantly, *why* you're saying it. But to say no, you first need to have a firm grasp of why you shouldn't say yes. The following paragraphs are things that you may have never heard before or might not agree with yet, but in the end, it will all make sense as to why you need to reset the relationship protocols you've adopted thus far and adopt an entirely new way of thinking.

Let's Talk About Your "No List"

What's a "No list"? It's a list of things that, as friends, should be off-limits to doing and/or saying. Things that must not happen while you are in the middle of growing close and deciding whether or not you will become exclusive with someone. Things that a large number of us do *every* time we meet someone and find ourselves attracted to them, or things that make us feel trapped because they are attracted to us and we have to cut them off. Things that cloud our judgment and distract us from making smarter choices. Things that trigger us and sling us into autopilot before we even know what's happening. This is not an all-exhaustive list, but it covers the major bases.

No going on "dates"

In the modern era with the rise of social media, vanity, easy access to sex, poor mental health, stress, and a myriad of other things, going on dates with someone is futile. Like I mentioned at the beginning of this book, any woman can dress up in her best outfit and do her makeup if necessary, and even the man at the bottom of the financial totem pole can scrape together a few dollars to rent a nice car and pay for a decent meal. Here's why it doesn't help.

While on dates, we highlight our best parts while severely hiding and suppressing our deepest flaws. When you are looking for someone to be with, you need to know things about them that simply will not get revealed until much, much later. If you are a woman and are looking for a protector and provider, then going on a date will *not* prove whether or not he is capable of being that for you. Likewise, if you are a man looking for a woman to be a helpmate and nurturer to you, then a date will not tell you whether she has a nasty attitude or has no idea how to speak life and encouragement into you.

While on a date, nothing of substance tends to get discussed. You have a limited amount of time to discover more about the person across the table from you, and while trying to accomplish this, you will avoid talking about issues that could be considered controversial or sensitive and you'll usually only cover superficial things like what your goals are or where you see yourself in five years. You won't talk about your insecurities or shortcomings, and you won't talk about your weaknesses or how you feel about things that could turn into dealbreakers.

While on a date, there is usually an unspoken agreement that the purpose of the date is to discover whether or not the person across the table *could* be your next relationship. This is *not* a good formula for success because the entire evening, you'll have expectations that will cause you to second-guess and overanalyze the way they act, what they say, and how they say it. You'll be too critical or not critical enough, and you'll be looking at what they do through your "date" lens instead of your "friend" lens.

Consider reserving the time, resources, and effort that you put into a date for someone that has demonstrated that they qualify for it. Otherwise, you end up with the frustrating yet easily avoidable disappointment of fixing yourself up for a date only to discover that the person sipping on a drink across from you couldn't be more wrong for you if they were getting paid to do so.

No Netflix and chill

Probably the easiest one on the list to understand, but the one that people can't seem to avoid. *No Netflix and chill* means exactly what it says. Stop going over to someone's apartment late at night on a weekend to watch tv shows in your sweats and eat pizza. We always tell ourselves that they're just a friend, or that nothing is going to happen because he or she isn't our type.

Then next thing you know there's more "chill" happening

than Netflix, and a month later you're unofficially together. Stop that shit! If someone invites you over for Netflix and chill, run as fast as you can. When you're trying to find that special someone to be with, why would you choose to put yourself in a position where sex or sexual activity is most likely to happen? Why would you allow the sexual tension to potentially begin to build between you and this person when we all know that sex too early can skew the outcome of relationships? Why would you be in another person's apartment late at night, relaxing on a couch alone?

Unless you just want to be friends with benefits (which isn't a good idea either), why would you put yourself in a position to choose incorrectly? No more Netflix and chill. That's a privilege reserved exclusively for your boyfriend or girlfriend.

A great alternative to the typical late night/date night/Netflix rendezvous is to invite someone to do regular things during regular hours. This might sound obvious, but doing things like grocery shopping, washing your car, going to the library, grabbing coffee, or working on a side hustle are things we might not consider. Why? Because it's not sexy. It's not flashy and exciting. It's just...regular.

However, it's those regular interactions that build rapport and fill the pool. It's those regular interactions that allow you to see who someone is in real, everyday situations. It's those regular interactions that are waiting for you on the other side of exclusivity. Having more of those now versus later is never a bad thing.

No introducing them to parents or family

If you are a guy and you introduce a male friend of yours to the family, it's usually not a big deal. But when you introduce someone of the opposite sex to the family, it carries a different weight. Whether or not you two are just friends isn't the point. The point is that unless this woman or man that you're getting to know is who you're going to claim as your partner in any capacity, there's no reason they need to meet your parents, your brother, your sister, your pastor, or your cousin who visits every other Thanksgiving.

Now, if you are with your friend and a member of your family happens to bump into you, then that's ok. But you are to never go out of your way to make sure that your family knows who this person is and is aware that he or she is in your life. It's completely unnecessary, it can give them opinions about him or her, and it might make your friend feel uncomfortable or give them the impression that you have a hidden agenda. Until you two get serious, keep the family out of it.

Instead, treat them like any other friend. Again, you must always remember that until you know enough information about this person to make a valid judgment call on whether or not you're compatible, they are just another friend. They may check the superficial boxes, but until they check the substantial ones, they get the same treatment.

No texting or calling them ten times a day

When you have chemistry with someone, it's easy to feel drawn to them. It's even easier to give them a call, and it's the easiest thing in the world to shoot them a quick text several times throughout the day. Here's a little piece of advice: *don't!* Think about people you are good friends with already. Maybe someone you met in college or a close cousin. Do you call or text them all day long? Do you text them good morning and good afternoon, and how was work, and hope dinner was good, and goodnight? Hell no, you don't.

So why on earth would you dedicate so much of your mental space to someone who hasn't proven that they're going to be in your life long term? How can you check in with them every three hours when you don't even know what you're getting yourself into yet? It's not a good look in any scenario.

If you feel a connection to someone, then a simple "how was your day?" is more than enough. When my wife and I were just friends, we reached a point when we were speaking with each other every single day, but we weren't always available for one another, and we definitely weren't spending several hours on the phone during each interaction. We both had lives to live and things to do. At times, we might have time for a five-minute phone conversation between appointments, or a quick text just to wish the other a great day or send good luck wishes before an important meeting.

What I learned is that developing a strong relationship of any kind isn't about dominating someone's time. It's about two people aligning themselves in a way that grants them the time to interact without hindering one another from doing what they need to do to live their life.

Remember, as attractive or as successful as this other person is, they are your "friend" until further notice. Don't treat them as more than they are, because you'll set yourself up for disappointment the same way you have in the past. Connect with them when you can, not whenever you can. There's a big difference.

THE 'NO' LIST

No to always being available

It's interesting how available we make ourselves when we meet someone new and we start to feel those familiar feelings of attraction and connection, even as just friends. If you like someone and share similar interests, you'll naturally want to spend more time with them either in person or over the phone.

However, there is power in being unavailable. Fighting the urge to seize every opportunity to spend time with someone is something most people have trouble with. If so-and-so calls, you will make sure you are available to pick up, or if they text then you'll respond immediately. If they want to grab lunch on Saturday, you'll do it even if you're not hungry or can't afford it, then you'll even regret it afterward. Why do we do this?

You have to understand that being unavailable is good for people. It's not healthy to always say yes to someone because the things that are done at the beginning of any relationship usually set the tone for things to come. It's in your best interest to communicate that although you enjoy speaking with them, you aren't always available, and it would be silly for them to expect that of you. What this does is create a healthy boundary that says to them, "Don't call me all the time because I might be busy, and more importantly, don't get mad if I don't respond right away." If she responds four days later, maybe she doesn't connect with you. But if it's just hours later, that's negligible.

No trying to impress

This one is *huge!* Impressing people can be a subtle thing we do, but when we make it a point to attempt to get someone's attention, we're already headed down the slippery slope of liking someone before knowing someone. This very quickly leads to setting expectations for something that hasn't even developed yet. Why would you be focused on trying to impress *anyone* before they've proven they deserve it?

At the end of the day, we only try to impress people we want something from because true friendship does not come with a hidden agenda. Do yourself a favor and skip trying to impress someone, because until you know who they are, how do you even know that you want what they have to give? How do you even know if being with them might be the one thing that sabotages your destiny and ruins your life? Fall back and just be yourself. If they are impressed by that, then more power to you.

Instead of trying to impress anyone, decide that what should impress them is *you*. Not a glorified representation of you. But the real you. Again, think back to your relationships that haven't gone the distance. They started off great, right? You may have won his or her heart, but in the end, the deciding factor was not what was done to impress each other, but who you two really were and what that looked like in the real world. Put a different way, trying to impress someone is similar to trumping up your resume and landing a job, only to discover that the job sucks and you wish you never made that decision. Don't just be good on paper. Be good in real life. And the best way to actually be good is to be yourself and let that be what draws people to you.

The "No list" is just a starting point. A quick-start guide into things that a lot of us do with our "friends" that we shouldn't be doing if the ultimate goal is to find a spouse. If you dig deep, you'll find that the quickest way to waste a few years of your life in a relationship that was headed nowhere from the beginning is to continue to fall back into the bad habits of our past. We have to be intentional about every single thing we do, and oftentimes, it means that no matter how tempting something or someone looks, we should just say no.

17

The 'Yes' List

So what can you do as someone who chooses to become friends first? I mean, you can't Netflix and chill, you can't call someone all day, every day, and you can't say yes to every single thing they invite you to. Well, despite these "drawbacks," employing Friends First is an incredible way to build relationships, free up your time and energy, and free you of the up and down of the dating rollercoaster.

Here's what should be on your "Yes list."

Yes to meeting more people

As we all know, once you cross the relationship threshold with someone, you will naturally spend less time with others who could be seen as potential mates. When you are friends first, you can meet and connect with as many people as you'd like, whenever you'd like. This doesn't mean you hit on everyone you meet or get as many phone numbers as you can. It means that when you meet someone and find common interests or a similar vibe, you can confidently ask if they'd like to connect at a future time, and you can do this often.

When we are single, we can sometimes find ourselves in the "find a mate" mentality where if someone we meet isn't a candidate, then they don't deserve our time in any capacity. We operate with an all-or-nothing approach. This is a fatal mistake. Remember that life happens out in the real world, and by making connections with people, you set yourself up for success in intimate as well as personal and professional relationships. That guy you met could be two degrees of separation away from the business funding you've been desperately searching for. That same guy could also introduce you to your husband next week had you taken the time to simply introduce yourself.

So say yes to meeting new people and meeting them often. It will serve you well.

Yes to being your true self

Once you get out in the real world, this is your chance to introduce people to the real you. The first part of this is saying yes to the notion that you can and should show up as who you really are. What does this mean? On one end of the spectrum, we have those who try to impress others, and this can lead to lying about who we are or what we've done, omitting things about who we are or what we've done, and on a basic level, not being completely honest about who we are, what we've been through, what we want, or where we're headed in life.

On the other end of the spectrum is a place where you are honest about who and what you are and, more importantly, make no excuses about it. You own it, and you understand that for others to connect with you in a real way, they will need to own it too.

What does this look like? It looks like not being afraid to tell people your truth. Mistakes you've made in past relationships, failures you've experienced in life, regrets, your worldviews about religion and politics, and much more. We tend to avoid what we deem "sensitive topics," but if you think about it, that doesn't really make sense.

Granted, when you first meet someone, you don't want to discuss the new abortion bill ad nauseam, *but* if and when that or other topics come up in conversation, you don't want to shy away from them. We will shy away from hot button issues because we don't want to cause an argument, but won't this argument happen anyway? I mean, you're never *not* going to talk about this stuff, right? So if that's the case, why should you feel like you can't speak on something?

The great thing about being friends first is that you are not attached to the outcome of any particular conversation or interaction with others because how you feel is how you feel. You want to connect with people who continue to enjoy your company in spite of a difference of opinion.

Showing up as your true self should be non-negotiable. It helps you find your tribe, it connects you to other like-minded individuals, and it helps others make a judgment call early on as to whether or not they'd like to develop a relationship in any capacity. And remember, this is what we want. We want strong, healthy relationships across the board moving forward, not superficial connections that can fall apart with a misplaced conversation.

THE 'YES' LIST

Yes to showing interest in people (the right way)

Yes! When you are Friends First–minded, it opens up the chance for you to show interest in people, but in a much healthier way. Before most people meet someone, it's through the lens of wondering whether or not they could be "the one" at some point, or whether or not they could have something of value to offer — not really interested in them, but interested in how they might satisfy an underlying relationship agenda. This might look like only talking to a woman if you're attracted to them physically or gravitating to someone you think makes the type of income you'd like your future spouse to make. Unfortunately, this type of "interest" we show people is disingenuous and is what causes us to fall into autopilot love or simply miss out on connecting with really great people.

When you meet someone, there shouldn't be an asterisk next to their name. Your intention after meeting someone should be to show interest in them and show it the right way. Just met someone who is a finalist in a pitch competition? Ask them how their journey has been up until this point and what they plan to do if they win — not because you think they might be able to help you, but because you are genuinely curious about how they made it to where they are. Just met someone who opened up a dance studio in LA? Offer to connect them with a friend who lives in the area who might be able to help them boost their client base — not because you want them to feel indebted to you or because you want to impress them, but because you genuinely want to see them win with no strings attached. Showing interest in people the right way is about directing your energy towards what that person is doing, not what that person could be doing for you if you push the right buttons.

Showing interest in people the right way will help you interact with others without wanting or needing something from them. There's nothing worse than giving off a thirsty vibe, whether it be in personal, intimate, or business relationships. People can pick up on that and it will turn them off. When you are able to network without always wanting something or having a hidden agenda in mind, you will always come out on top. People will see you call or message and not run from the interaction, but welcome it. Why? Because they know you aren't coming in the door with your hand out.

Say yes to showing interest in others for all the right reasons, and watch your relationships grow, both in quantity and quality.

Yes to walking away

This is a big one. Listen and listen closely. Walking away is so much easier as a friend than as a lover. *Period.* There's simply no comparison to the amount of pain you will avoid when you are able to approach relationships in a way that both protects you and allows you to get to know others in a healthy way while giving you the ability to walk away if necessary. It's much easier said than done to walk away from a relationship because feelings, emotions, and time have been invested.

But walking away from a friendship is not only less painful; it's just so simple. There's no "conversation" that needs to happen and there's no guilt that comes along with it, either. If you have connected with someone and they have done something that indicates they may not be on the same page as you in ways that are important to you, then simply walk away.

Yes! Walking away is something you can look forward to as opposed to diving into something and suffering more injuries.

No, walking away in this capacity will not leave you as bitter, hurt, resentful, or angry. It will help you understand more about what you are looking for in relationships of all kinds and will leave you better equipped to connect with others in the future. No, you won't have to invest a dominant portion of your time, energy, and resources to get to this point, as opposed to what you would have done had you been exclusive. Yes, you will still be able to continue learning and growing as a result.

Walking away as a friend can change your life for the better, as you'll still learn important lessons about life without all of the battle scars. Walk away as a friend before you make the mistake of getting in too deep and needing to walk away as something more.

Say yes to love when the time is right

After meeting and making connections with people from all walks of life, showing up as your true self, being honest about what you've been through and where you are in life, showing genuine interest in others in the right way, and walking away from those that don't add value to your life, you will undoubtedly put yourself into position to build a connection with someone that could turn into a lifetime of happiness. And when that happens...say yes. Say *yes!* The beautiful thing about being friends first is that all parties involved are learning and growing together, and once you reach a point where you feel as though a spark could be there, it is not only your duty but your obligation to say yes! You must say yes. You have taken the time to get to know this person and have done it in a healthy, fulfilling way. Saying yes is the last step and the most important.

At this point, you can't get cold feet or begin to doubt what it is that you're feeling. You should have weeks, months, and possibly years of data that reinforce the feelings that you have, and that's why you have to say yes. Think about it. You've done the work. You've been patient. You haven't fallen victim to your triggers. You have stood by while the pool filled up. This isn't like all of the other times. You know what you're getting yourself into and it shouldn't feel like a risk at all. It should feel like a natural, logical next step towards a more exclusive relationship with someone who you know on a genuine, authentic level.

How you say yes is something we'll talk about soon, but it's not up for debate whether or not you should say yes. For all the times you've ever said yes without knowing what you should have, this is the one time you should say yes and say it with confidence. This is what you've been waiting for. This is what you've been hoping for. Say yes to love when the time is right.

This "Yes list" is not a five-step process to success in meeting someone — it's a blueprint for life. The goal is to build healthy relationships by saying yes and saying yes to the right things. When you are able to do that consistently, then you give yourself the best chance at not only finding people to do life with but finding that one person to do life with forever.

18

The Shift

I was engaged, paying bills, shared bank accounts, had a child, and was living with someone who wasn't right for me. I was in deep. After that relationship ended, I was sitting in my apartment one day reliving all of the stress, anger, and regret of making the wrong choice in partner; of ignoring red flags; and of dealing with the pain of knowing I could not get the time, money, and energy back from almost six years of going in the wrong direction. As I sat there, thinking of this relationship and the others before it that failed, a voice popped in my head that I heard clear as day.

> "Jerrell. It's your fault. You don't
> know how to choose the right woman."

I sat there in silence as I let that statement sink in. As I began to take a deeper look, I realized that regardless of the outcome of the failed relationships and regardless of who was right or wrong, I was to blame for all of it because I chose the wrong person. It doesn't matter if I was young or naïve, or if I didn't have the guidance and knowledge that could have led to different choices. I was to blame. Period.

It was at that moment that something changed inside of me. Instead of sulking or beating myself up over past mistakes, I accepted the reality that I was completely incapable of choosing the right woman. I made up in my mind that from that point forward, I would never allow myself to begin something if I wasn't sure that it would be able to go the distance. I made the shift.

The shift is a subtle, life-changing alteration in how you determine when it's safe to enter into a new relationship with someone. It will help you decide when you say yes to allowing someone else to have access to all of the best parts of you. It helps you decide when, and more importantly, why you think another person is qualified to receive all the benefits of having you in their life exclusively.

The shift is a paradigm change that says the following.

- I will *not* enter into an exclusive relationship with someone until we are friends first.
- I will *not* enter into a relationship before I believe that this person could not only be my boyfriend or girlfriend but my spouse.
- I will *never* give someone the benefit of the doubt until they have proven they deserve the best of me.
- I will *not* put a time limit on how long it takes to discover if someone is right for me.
- I will ask the hard questions on the front end and *not* the back end.

- I will *not* set expectations for anyone without knowing the facts about them.
- I will *not* ignore the red flags, ever.
- I will *not* try to impress anyone in the hopes that they will like me in return.
- I will *not* be afraid to lose anyone who does not add value to my life.
- I will be *honest* with myself about what I want first before requiring honesty from others.
- I will approach relationships with a fact-finding mentality and stay neutral throughout the entire friendship process.

When you make the shift, triggers become your best friend and ultimately become the cornerstone of how you gauge when it's time to dive in and when it's time to hold back. When you make the shift, you can view triggers not as reasons to say "yes," but as reasons to say, "Let's take a closer look." This shift is what pushes you into a space of putting more emphasis on knowing and less on feeling. If your relationship is emotionally top-heavy, there's no way to guarantee it will stand the test of time until all hell breaks loose in the form of arguments, disagreements, and mistakes. What allows a couple to go the distance is compatibility, not just love. Or rather, love that has developed because of compatibility, and not just because of time or trauma.

"Commitment before compatibility breeds failure."

A trigger can be your worst enemy or your best friend depending on how you handle the information, and the shift is the best chance you have at discerning how to move forward once your spider-sense goes off.

19

Q & A

After understanding the Friends First approach to finding someone, I know you have a lot of questions. This is a good thing. Here is where we bring everything full circle and connect all the dots. Below you'll find answers to a lot of the things you may be wondering at this point.

How do I become Friends First with someone who wants more? - That's the beauty of becoming friends first. It allows you to see situations and people for what they really are up front and not on the other side of commitment. One thing you should always keep in mind is the fact that by choosing to become friends first, you are positioning yourself for the long game, and if someone is interested in temporary satisfaction or fly-by-night fun, you can choose not to subscribe.

This does not mean you give everyone the cold shoulder. It simply means that the people you do meet are given the same amount of consideration, and those who do not qualify will be looked over. You will, however, connect with people on the same wavelength as you. It's inevitable. You need not worry about when — you must simply ensure that you are putting your best foot forward when you come into contact with others.

Remember that being friends first is not something you need to announce or declare at the beginning of a relationship. It's simply something you need to adopt and keep in mind when you are meeting others. People who are in sync with that will be drawn to you naturally and vice versa. Being friends first is also not something that should dissolve a friendship if you find yourself in a situation where someone is interested in you on a level that you aren't ready for. You just need to communicate that at the moment, you aren't sure you know enough about them to feel comfortable being more than friends. This way, you can continue to enjoy each other's company without things potentially becoming awkward. And at the end of it all, if you and someone else are not on the same page, you can always choose to remove them from your life.

How do I know when the pool is full? - The pool is full when you say it is. The problem a lot of us run into is that we either dive in when we know for a fact it's empty or *we think* the pool is full when it's really not. Before you verify that the pool is full, make sure your interpretation of a full pool is up to date with how you now understand relationships. Some of us have an outdated idea of what a healthy relationship should or could look like and thus jump in when it's still not safe.

Take time to reflect on the things you need to see from a mate that would make you truly happy, and make sure that you know which questions to ask and what information you absolutely need to know before you dive in. This is different for each and every individual, but if you have the right information in mind and someone provides that over the course of time, then consider the pool to be at a safe level and enjoy the swim.

Is it possible to wait too long before becoming more than friends? - Yes and no. No in the sense that you can never learn too much about a person, as the goal is always to gather the most information possible before making a decision. Yes in the fact that you don't want to wait five-plus years, as that could be enough time for someone to meet someone else, get to know them, and get married. How long does it take to become friends first? There's no perfect number, but it doesn't take *that* long. As with most things in life, use your best judgment. If you don't think you know enough about someone to make a permanent decision, then don't. If you think you know enough, by all means, express your desire to become more.

How do I let someone know that I want to be more than friends? - This is a million-dollar question, but it's not as complicated as you think. When you've taken the time to get to know someone in the right way and you've started to feel like they could be a good candidate for a committed relationship, how do you let them know your intentions?

In all honesty, you just tell them. It doesn't even necessarily have to be a grand occasion. You can simply call them up or invite them for coffee and let them know how you really feel. The best part is that if they are your real friend, you should be able to tell them this without feeling weird or awkward. As an added thought, a lot of times the feelings that we are experiencing are mutual and will be met with a warm response. If done correctly, you should have a deep understanding of what their likes and dislikes are in a potential partner, and they should give you a better idea of whether or not your advance, for lack of a better term, will be accepted.

After my wife and I were friends for as long as we were, we actually shared a kiss when I went to visit her. However, instead of flinging ourselves into a relationship right away, we candidly spoke about whether or not a relationship even made sense for over three months before we were officially together. What I enjoyed the most was the fact that it really didn't make anything different between us. Instead of things becoming weird, we continued to be honest about what we were really feeling, and after going over the details, we decided to move forward. Today we are enjoying life as husband and wife.

When it comes right down to it, if you feel as though you have to speak on it, *speak on it.* This goes back to saying yes to love. Say yes!

How do I meet more people? - Before you can meet people, you need to put yourself in a position to meet those people. If I asked you to write a schedule of your daily activity for a week, what would it consist of? For a lot of people, it could comprise of waking up, eating breakfast, drinking coffee, going to work, going home, eating dinner, and watching tv before falling asleep. For those who get out on the weekends, your schedule might include waking up late, running errands, hanging out with the same friends that you always do at a lot of the same places, and staying up late to drink, eat bad food, or do something somewhat social. The point is that your life does not make room for you to meet new people. We need to fix this.

To meet more people, there are a few things you can do:

1. Do new activities and go to new places more often. This

is the easiest way to meet more people. Go somewhere you normally don't go. Farmer's markets, social gatherings, fundraisers, galas, paint and sips, yoga classes, community events, grand openings, and more. There is always something going on, and all you need to do is plug into the energy that's moving around your city. If there's something you'd like to do but don't see it happening, start it yourself. Get active where you are.

2. Introduce yourself to more people. If you introduced yourself to just one person a day, that's 365 new people you would have met in just a year. A simple, "Hey, how's your day going?" or, "Good morning, do you come here often?" is all it takes to start a conversation that could lead to a great friendship or potentially more. Don't become thirsty for meeting new people in the process, and don't introduce yourself to every single person you come in contact with. The point is to simply introduce yourself to more people than you currently do.

Introducing yourself is a great way to add quality people to your life and potentially meet that special someone. It's something you should definitely focus on moving forward.

If I'm older, should I still choose to become friends first? - If you are older, then you may feel as though you are running out of time. It's at this point, however, that you don't want to make any rash decisions or rush into anything. Granted, the older you are, the deeper an understanding you should have of yourself and what you are looking for in a partner. Thus, you might be able to arrive at the decision to embark on a new relationship a bit quicker than when you were younger. But this does not erase the fact that you still need to get to know others before you make that decision.

20

Love On Purpose

There's no worse feeling than waking up the morning after a breakup wondering what in the hell happened, and on the other end of the spectrum, there is no greater feeling than waking up knowing that you want to spend the rest of your life with somebody. The difference is knowing how to choose the right person. The difference is being patient and understanding the importance and weight of this one single decision. The difference is not looking for love but looking for someone compatible.

The difference between experiencing your lowest low or your highest high is simply having the burning desire to make sure that the person you give the best parts of yourself to deserves it. The difference is both in what you do and what you don't do. The difference really and truly is in whether or not you become friends first.

Being friends first does something that changes the game as far as finding that special someone is concerned, and that's giving you the confidence to love on purpose. Traditionally, once we take the deep dive with someone, a lot of us typically move forward with no clear-cut game plan, or at least the default game plan which entails figuring things out along the way. But the side effect of this is two-fold.

1. Figuring things out along the way is a surefire way to waste years of your life because as soon as you discover a dealbreaker, it's a wrap.
2. When or if you do decide that getting married makes sense, it can often be because you two have simply just been together for a while. It's been several years and getting married "just makes sense" for you two.

This is a tragedy waiting to happen.

When you are friends first, it gives you the unique opportunity to love someone on purpose because you know that they are right for you. Not in a honeymoon phase kind of way, but in an "I know them on a very deep, personal level that gives me the confidence to give them my love because I know they deserve it" kind of way. There's a big difference. We already know how serious love and marriage are, and when you can clear the major hurdles before giving your love away, it makes loving easier, more exciting, and more enjoyable.

The days of hoping someone marries you or the days of wondering if someone is right for you are gone. If you can become friends first, love will take care of itself naturally and will help you to love on purpose and not just because of proximity. You should *never* convince yourself that you love someone just because you've been with them for a few years.

Then you've participated in a soft form of just settling. Love should not be a result of convenience.

Ask yourself if you've ever loved on purpose, or if you loved someone simply because they were around. Ask yourself why you can never seem to give yourself fully to someone without feeling worried or hesitant. Ask yourself why your partner never wants to talk about marriage or changes the subject when you talk about long-term plans.

The answer to all of these questions is easy. They aren't sure what they are giving themselves to. They aren't loving on purpose. When you know for a fact that the person you are with is the *right* person, you will give yourself to that person effortlessly. No reservations. No exceptions. No fine print. When you know that the person you're with is worthy of your love, they will never have to twist your arm or convince you to give it to them. *That* is what loving on purpose feels like, and that's why being friends first is so very important.

21

Change

As humans, we all want to feel a sense of progress. We want to feel as though we have a handle on our lives and that even though we have ups and downs, we still have it all figured out. It's that optimism that helps us to achieve our greatest accomplishments and stay focused on the future. We have to understand, however, that the most crucial element involved in making progress in life is embracing change. Change is the only thing that helps us to reach our highest highs and harness our skills to be more and do more. If we want more, we *have* to change. It's one of the things in life that you cannot get around. We've all heard the famous quote….

If you want something you've never had, you have to do something you've never done."

This quote is great, but if you break it down to the core of the message, that quote says one simple thing.

If you want better, change.

Change as if your life depends on it, because nothing in life stays constant. The weather changes, your weight changes, the value of a dollar changes, and on and on it goes. And if you don't change with it, then you will be left to pick up the pieces while those who adapt and adjust will reap the rewards. Toys "R" Us, Sears, K-Mart, and a list of other conglomerates have gone bankrupt in the last five years alone simply because they didn't adapt to the times. It's a stark reminder that the inability to change can cost you everything.

Relationships tend to be a sore spot for many of us because many people are unwilling to look themselves in the mirror and ask what they could be doing better. I've discovered that one of the hardest things to do as a person is to admit when you are wrong or to simply admit you need help. No one, and I mean no one, wants to accept the weight of all their bad decisions, and no one likes to look back on their life only to realize how wrong they've been. But the only way you can move forward is by first being honest and acknowledging exactly where you are. Look yourself in the mirror and be brutally honest about why things have transpired the way they have. Be so honest that it hurts, and then be honest some more. Dig until you hit the root of the problem.

If you fall in love very quickly and fall out just as quickly, then you need to change. If you suffered heartbreak after heartbreak but have no sense of direction as to how to avoid the next one, then you need to change. If everyone you date tends to fall in the same category of being superficial, manipulative, reluctant to commit, and disingenuous, then at the core of everything, you need to change. If you have suffered trauma and realize that it may be the thing that is keeping you from seeing success in your relationships, you need to change.

This isn't an indictment of you as a person, nor is it a personal attack, but the common denominator in every single relationship you've ever had is undoubtedly you. And whether it was what you did to attract the other person or the behaviors you exhibited, you played a part in the relationship's success or failure. Only by realizing this can you then take the steps necessary to address what you can do to make sure that the next person you invite into your life will be the right person.

At this point, you are feeling one of two things:

1. This book is the answer to your prayers. It spoke to you in a way other books haven't, and you feel excited about how to move forward.
2. This book is just more fluff, and you feel no different than you did before opening the first page.

Regardless of how you feel, my only hope is that the concepts and ideas in this book have made you think. Thinking leads to seeing things from a different perspective. Seeing things from a different perspective leads to seeking answers, and seeking answers is what leads to change. Change is what we're after. Change is what makes you choose differently than you have in the past, and change is the catalyst for a different outcome than what you typically experience.

Right now, there are so many people in pain, so many people wanting to find love so badly but not knowing how or where to even start. I want you to know that all is not lost, but only if you are willing to change the way you approach this thing. Now that you have a new way of thinking, what are you going to do with it? Will you take action? Will you ask yourself the hard questions and be honest about where you are and how you got there, or will you fall back into the same pattern of behavior that has landed you where you are? The choice is yours.

I hope that after reading this book, you've reevaluated your position on what it means to embark on a serious relationship, you've come to terms with what part you've played in the shortcomings you've experienced, and you are clear on what you have to do win the next time around.

Take the information you've gained and run with it. Share it with others. Talk about it. Dissect it. Disagree with it. Look at it again and again. Do whatever you want with it, but please, please don't stay the same. Don't continue to do the same things you've always done and find yourself on the other side of heartbreak again.

Whatever you do, I hope that you'll choose to be friends first.

Bonus Chapter

Part of getting relationships right is asking more questions and asking better questions. Below you'll find 30 questions you can ask TODAY to jumpstart your journey to getting to know the people in your life. Ask, respond, reflect, and grow.

1. Have you ever told someone that you don't need them?
2. Do you listen to respond, or do you listen to understand? Do you know the difference between the two?
3. Do the divorce rates motivate you to find the right partner, or do they make you pessimistic about the potential dangers of marriage?
4. Do you believe in soulmates?
5. What does a healthy marriage look like to you?
6. Does voting work? Explain in detail why or why not.
7. Would you rather finance a car now or save up for 3 years to buy in cash?
8. What is the one thing in life you must accomplish before you leave this earth?
9. If you checked your bank balance right now and it said $0, what is the very FIRST thing you would do?
10. If you won the lottery and received a lump sum of 100 million dollars tonight, what is the first thing you would do tomorrow morning?
11. What is the best age to get married and why?

12. Do you believe in divorce? Explain your answer.
13. What does the term "submit" mean to you?
14. What is the best way to discipline your kids?
15. Would you rather be 15 minutes early and not fully prepared, or would you rather be 15 minutes late and be fully prepared?
16. What is the perfect number of children to have?
17. Is marriage necessary anymore?
18. How does the trauma you've experienced in life affect your behavior today?
19. How long after a relationship should you take before you embark on a new one?
20. How do you react when you don't get your way?
21. Name three things you have accomplished in the last 6 months.
22. How long should it take a man to propose to a woman he loves?
23. If you fall out of love, were you ever in love to begin with?
24. Would you rather be single for 10 years or go through 2 bad breakups in 10 years?
25. What has been a pattern you have observed in most or all of your serious relationships?
26. What's one thing you're afraid to tell people you don't know how to do?
27. You can only pick one to have for the rest of your life: driver's license or passport. Which do you choose and why?
28. What's the most traumatic experience you've ever had?
29. Fill in the blank: One thing I want to be remembered for is _____.
30. Is YOUR glass currently half full or half empty?

About the Author

After missing out on true love for over a decade, Jerrell decided it was time for a change. He shifted his priorities and found his wife and soulmate Rebecca.

Jerrell is an author, international wedding & event photographer, notary, husband, and father currently living in Austin, Texas.

You can connect with me on:
🌐 https://www.jerrelltrulove.com

Subscribe to my newsletter:
✉ https://www.jerrelltrulove.com/newsletter

Made in the USA
Monee, IL
23 June 2022